TO SHERRI,

Who put on every hat
I handed her

and some I didn't.

CONTENTS

WHO THE FUCK AM I
(AND WHO THE FUCK ARE YOU)? - 6

WHAT THE FUCK IS TAROT? - 12

WHAT THE FUCK IS MAGIC? - 16

HOW THE FUCK DO I CHOOSE A DECK? - 19

THE MAJOR ARCANA - 23

THE MINOR ARCANA - 77

THE COURT CARDS - 103

WHAT THE FUCK ARE TAROT SPREADS? - 119

HOW THE FUCK DO I GIVE A READING? - 124

Tarot FAQ for Noobs - 125

Daily Draw - 128

The Shitty Cards - 129

The Cards in Relationship - 130

Reversed Cards - 131

Boundary Setting & Energetic Protection - 132

Dealing with Assholes - 135

ENHANCING YOUR MAGIC - 138

Chakras - 139

Crystals - 142

Meditation and Intuition - 143

Building Altars - 145

Journaling - 147

Space Clearing - 148

IT'S BEEN REAL (AND SURREAL) - 151

Acknowledgments - 152

About the Author and Illustrator - 153

Index - 154

WHO THE FUCK AM I? (AND WHO THE FUCK ARE YOU?)

I have been reading tarot professionally for a little over four years, which is not a particularly impressive number. It is not a number that implies a lifetime of devotion and study in the same way that *four decades* might. It is enough time to acquire an undergraduate degree, which barely qualifies you for a babysitting job these days. And yet, in these short four years, I have built a full-time tarot practice, offered intensive group and individual trainings, facilitated workshops, taught classes, opened a retail store and healing space, created a tarot deck and, now, written a book on the damn thing.

If someone had told me that, in order to read tarot, I needed to join a monastery, spend a year in silent meditation, apprentice under a more established tarot reader for a few more years and then pass a rigorous exam at the end, that would have made much more sense to me than the swift, uncomplicated way tarot came into my life and changed absolutely everything.

Maybe that is why the "Who the fuck am I?" question comes up so strongly for people who are drawn to the tarot. There are no quantifiable tests, formal qualifications or degrees to frame and hang on the wall. You can study the cards, certainly, and you should. But what I have come to believe about the tarot is that there is something at the core of our souls, in the marrow of our bones, that recognizes these images, archetypes and energies. The experiences and emotions captured by the cards, while steeped in myth and symbolism, are universal.

When someone meets the tarot for the first time, there is often a spark of recognition because the cards function as a mirror. The longing we feel to connect with them is the longing we feel to connect with the truest version of ourselves and others. The tarot is your most honest friend, the one who loves you enough to call you out on your shit. Who can hear you tell a story and strip down the exaggeration and bravado and ego and see you clearly. We've all offered this to a person we love, probably without using cards, at some point. The tarot is a tool that allows us to provide this clarity to anyone, including strangers and ourselves.

Standing at the beginning of my journey with the tarot, I felt an immediate connection to the cards. I was also totally overwhelmed and a little bit paralyzed by the "Who the fuck am I?" question. The only indication that I had any spiritual inclinations was my lifelong Harry Potter obsession (but trust that is a very intense, full-blown, arguably problematic one) and an affinity for the astrology section of magazines. I do not come from a magical lineage. I wasn't initiated by the elders of my spiritual community—unless hallucinogenic drugs count—and while I thought esotericism was fascinating, I was also deeply skeptical of it. I owned a few crystals, but only because I found them in bookshops and thought they were beautiful. I had no idea what the tarot was.

Sure I watched Matilda when I was younger and tried really hard to move objects with my mind like any self-respecting millennial child. Maybe I read a middle-grade mystery novel about a girl who astral projected all over the world and spent years trying to peel my consciousness from my body like an irrelevant but stubborn shadow. The day after my mother passed away when I was six years old, I dreamt that she walked out of my bathroom, glowing in white light, sat down on the foot of my bed and talked to me for ten minutes. But growing up has a way of beating your belief in magic out of you. When I received my first tarot deck, I was twenty-three years old and had very little memory of my magical predilections and even less interest in reconnecting with them. I was a new-to-Brooklyn little whippersnapper fresh out of college and about a year into my first adult job, where I had to put on real clothes and go into an office every day.

I studied publishing in school and landed a job at a literary agency in Manhattan's Flatiron district. Housed in an old brownstone, it contained the charm of a converted residence and the mystery of a very old building. Former bathrooms-turned-tiny-offices for junior agents, hand-hewn woodwork and ornate stained glass, a massive vault in the back office of the ground floor that revealed the building's banking history. Accessible only by a narrow winding staircase, my office was a sunlit attic room. The company was small and full of characters—most of them decent, incredibly hardworking, fiercely intelligent people. The place was magic in its own right, and landing a job there felt like winning the lottery.

Like any self-respecting millennial adolescent, I was also in therapy. In addition to a pretty horrific childhood that guaranteed lifetime admission to the "needing therapy" club, I was quickly promoted in aforementioned adult job and while my ego was flying high on that achievement, my nervous system had other ideas about it. At the suggestion of a dear friend and author at my agency, I started with a new therapist a couple months before. A raven haired, impossibly beautiful goddess-of-an-older-woman named Sherri. Her office was a bright corner room overlooking 28th Street that always smelled like gardenias and white sage. The only objects in it were a simple mid-century armchair where she sat, a light gray couch where her clients sat, a shelf in the corner that showcased books, trinkets, crystals and—I would soon learn—several tarot decks. There was a huge foam cube in the corner that, when strong emotions were evoked during a session, Sherri would encourage her clients to beat the shit out of with a tennis racket and scream. She practiced a form of body-based psychotherapy that folds in the spiritual element.

At the time, I called this "the weird hippie therapy that I do." Now, I understand the importance of intuition and the mind-body-spirit connection when it comes to healing a person.

For the first few months, sessions with Sherri were made up of me whining about my job, managing the stress of adult life and unpacking my poor life decisions regarding finances, sleeping habits and men. Occasionally she would try to steer me into the murky waters of my childhood, which was a tactic that after a decade and a half in therapy I was able to detect and avoid with ease. I refused any of the bodywork or physical exercises she suggested. I never cried.

Every Monday morning at 7 a.m. (AKA the worst hour of the whole week probably) I would come into Sherri's office in a blaze of glory, massive coffee in hand, armed with the list of that week's issues.

On this particular morning, however, Sherri asked me something before I got a chance to take out my list.

"I just bought a tarot deck for someone as a gift. Do you want to see it?"

Why on earth this woman thought I would want to see a tarot deck, I don't know. But she took the deck out of her bag and handed it to me.

As soon as the cards hit my hands, I started to weep.

The response was so immediate and so visceral; there was no thought or decision to start crying. Tears were forcing themselves from my eyeballs before I even properly looked at the box holding the cards. I couldn't explain what was going on. It felt like meeting someone you loved, but somehow forgot you knew. It felt like remembering.

We sat like that for a long time, me crying softly, holding this plastic-wrapped box of cards like a baby bird.

When I eventually stopped, she said in a very matter-of-fact way, "You need to take these cards. They're yours."

"What the fuck am I going to do with them?" was all I could manage.

I am refraining from a more dramatic retelling, but if it were up to me I would cue some epic Titanic-esque music and invoke some receiving-the-tablets-on-the-mountain imagery. I have thought about this pivotal morning a thousand times. I've picked Sherri's brain over and over again, trying to bottle the moment she decided to bring up the tarot, to put it in a test tube over a flame and extract its individual ingredients. I wonder where I would be, what my life would look like, had she not listened to her intuition and put that deck in my hands. I recall the series of synchronistic events that led me to that morning and feel humbled and awed and small and grateful.

A few weeks later, a stranger by the name of Lisa contacted me for a reading, asking about things like availability and rates. S'cume? The "Who the fuck am I?" question hit me like a ton of bricks. I definitely did not feel ready to read for another person. I hadn't joined a monastery or found a place to silently meditate for a million years yet. I was too young, too unprepared, too inexperienced, too sarcastic, too non-magical to give a reading to anyone. I told her this.

Lisa was stubborn. She insisted she trusted the person who referred her to me (fucking Sherri) and that she felt strongly about getting a reading specifically from me. I panicked, but agreed to see her. I tried to become an expert on the tarot in the couple days between her contacting me and our scheduled meeting via extensive Internet searches, but that was a depressing and disheartening endeavor. Every source interpreted the cards differently. The tarot is a complicated esoteric object, used across cultures and in different spiritual contexts for centuries. There are hundreds of lenses through which one can study the tarot, and even if I chose one, it was far more information than could be absorbed in two days. This was when I still believed memorization and a cognitive grasp of the cards was what was needed to be an effective tarot reader.

I gave up. If I made an idiot of myself in front of this stranger, it wouldn't be the first (or the worst) time.

While I didn't know much, I felt a connection to the tarot as well as a shift within myself since receiving my deck. I started meditating the night I got them, visualizing myself in the scenes each card depicted in order to further explore them. I played around with pulling cards for friends. My dreams grew vivid and unfamiliar. I started reading about the tarot's history and individual card meanings a bit. The feeling of remembering grew. More than any of that, my longing to connect with these cards and the inherent magic I sensed in them was pervasive. They answered a question I didn't know I was asking, showed me something I had absolutely no clue I was looking for.

Lisa came over and sat on the couch and I sat on a chair in my little Brooklyn apartment. I pulled cards for her on my coffee table. I didn't consult a guidebook or outside resource. I don't know how much time passed. What I felt as I was reading for her was that while I didn't know anything about this person, the cards seemed to know exactly where she had been, where she was now and where she was going. I didn't worry about being right. The cards laid out a path and I gave a voice to the story they told. It was one of the most effortless, simple things I've ever done—easier than small talk. It was also one of the most profound and the most moving.

After the reading, Lisa hugged me, forced a fifty-dollar bill into my hand and left. I've seen her half a dozen times since, read for members of her family and cried to her in gratitude for forcing me into the most incredible journey of my life.

Six months and over a hundred clients later, I left my real job to read tarot full-time. This was a decision made after two straight weeks of leaving my office at five and giving readings until around midnight. My roommate wasn't into it, so readings took place in the small amount of floor space in my bedroom, sandwiched between my bed and closet. I was working more and harder than I'd ever worked in my life, but there was also a distinct sense of ease and flow to that period. Doors kept opening. People kept coming for readings. The answer was a continuous, resounding *yes*.

If four years is not an impressive number, then six months is a drop in the bucket. All the while I was wrestling with my feelings of inadequacy, legitimacy and worthiness to do this work. The "Who the fuck am I?" question kept me up at night. But what happened was with each day, each reading, each experience to help another person that the tarot afforded me, the question started to answer itself. I learned the "Who the fuck am I?" question is a universal one. Who the fuck am I to think I deserve fulfilling, equal partnership? Who the fuck am I to have a job that I love? To demand respect, to be heard, to set boundaries, to believe that I can live a big, gorgeous, magical life?

The answer kept coming, for me and for my clients. You are a child of the divine, you are compressed stardust, you are a human being. You have a responsibility to cause as little harm to yourself and others as possible. To live the best, biggest life you can and to leave everyone you come across better than you found them.

I'm going to make what may be a radical declaration: You do not need to learn the tarot because you already know it. You may need to learn more about yourself, you may need to spend some time in the voluminous caverns of your own heart, but you do not need to memorize the textbook meanings of seventy-eight cards. Getting to know the tarot is identifying the times in your life when you have been in the presence of an archetype. When you took a huge risk and didn't know why you were doing it but only knew you must—that's The Fool. When you came to a crushing moment of clarity and asked "Wait, am I really still doing this shit?" you were in the presence of The Wheel of Fortune. When you let go of a relationship with someone you loved but knew you needed to leave, you were leaning into Death. When you had an overwhelming feeling that you were exactly where you need to be, doing exactly what you should be doing, you were embodying the energy of Judgment.

You know the essence of each card. There is also a lot you don't know. The tarot has been studied and interpreted through the lens of Gnosticism, Hermeticism, Kabbalah, astrology, alchemy, numerology, symbology, Wicca … just to name a few. There are tons of books on all of them, and they are valuable and rich resources for deepening your relationship with the cards. That is not this book. I know very little about most of those topics. I saw the cards, and I recognized them as a set of images that serves to identify the archetypes living in all of us. I believe that this soul-level recognition can happen between anyone who truly has a desire to connect with the cards and, by extension, their intuition. This is true of any deck of cards that you find personally resonant, and this book is written to guide you through any and all of them. Whether you want to use the cards for yourself, with your loved ones, or desire reading professionally, it is my hope that this book will convince you that you already have all you need to begin.

The "Who the fuck am I?" question rarely comes up for me anymore. I've answered it, for myself, in my dark nights of the soul, over and over again. I feel it sometimes—when I'm reading for an especially intimidating client, when I taught my first class on the tarot, when I was asked to write this book. But it doesn't plague me anymore. It doesn't roll around in my stomach like a pinball hitting every wormhole of self-doubt and self-hate in the way it once did. While the tarot is the thing that brought about the "Who the fuck am I?" question more intensely than any other fact of my life, it is also the thing that answered it.

And now I'm a full-time tarot card reader and healer. My clients are entrepreneurs, students, CEOs of major corporations, waiters, celebrities, stay-at-home moms, artists, other healers and a lot of people who don't know what the fuck they're doing. A lot of them use the tarot now in some capacity. Some pull a card for themselves every morning. Some of them bought a deck and stare it at from time to time. Some are full-time tarot readers. They've also asked the "Who the fuck am I" question and are answering it for themselves.

The voice of this book will be light, crass and hopefully funny, but do not let that be confused with nonchalance for the tarot itself. It changed my life in every way possible, and my intention is to make this incredible tool accessible to anyone interested in connecting with it.

As long as the tarot is shrouded in shadow and mystery, it is not being used to its full capacity. And that's who the fuck I am—your young blood, no-nonsense, sometimes sassy girl guide to this expansive and profound magical object. Don't freak out. Don't get overwhelmed. Don't feel like you're not in the cool kids club of people who are worthy of using these cards because they are somehow more magical or capable than you. You got this. Now let's fucking go.

WHAT THE FUCK
IS TAROT?

Simply put, the tarot is a deck of seventy-eight cards. It is believed that the whole spectrum of potential human experience is captured within these cards. The cards you pull at any given time speak to the experience you are having in that moment. Therefore, the meanings of the cards range from as dark and mysterious as our dreamscapes and shadow selves to as boring and adult-ish as saving money and not sleeping with that guy-you-really-want-to-sleep-with-but-know-it's-a-terrible-idea.

To add another sparkly layer of magic to this object, the origin of the tarot is unknown. Occultists' theories vary, and widely. From Ancient Greece and Egypt to Old Testament times, Atlantis and outer space—there is much speculation, but no proof, of where the tarot was born. It has been linked to the Kabbalistic tree of life, Dionysus, Pythagoras, Chaldean astrology, various initiatory rituals and the Romany people.

Where myth ends and fact begins is in the mid-fifteenth century, with the Visconti-Sforza family, who ruled Milan at the time. Now known as the Visconti tarot, it was most likely commissioned by an artist named Bonifacio Bembo as a wedding gift and intended as—no shit—a card game. In fact, the first written record of the tarot as a possibly divinatory and esoteric object came over three hundred freaking years later by this French dude and Freemason named Antoine Court de Gébelin. The tarot card game, referred to as Tarrochi in Italy, made its way to France under the name les Tarots. Court de Gébelin saw the cards and discerned them as visual distillations of the secrets of the Egyptian God Thoth.

From there, the cards were taken and interpreted by several occultists and esoteric societies over the next two centuries. Most notably, the Hermetic Order of the Golden Dawn, which spawned fantastic weirdos like Aleister Crowley, the creator of the Thoth Tarot Deck, and Arthur Edward Waite, who penned the most widely used and recognized modern tarot deck, published in London in 1909. The first deck to depict each card as a scene, or a moment in a story, the Rider Waite extended the tarot's reach beyond these boys-club secret societies and birthed the contemporary tarot interpretation.

Personally, I do not at all believe that the tarot's first manifestation was as a deck of playing cards for some Milanese noble family. It seems much more likely that some gnarled Egyptian mystic rocking fierce malachite eye shadow went into trance and woke up with this set of images, channeled directly from the cosmos. But does it matter? What an amazing thing that the tarot has been claimed across cultures, creeds and continents. That it is so universally resonant that it can be plausibly connected to so many different origins. That it has endured and stayed relevant for at least six and a half centuries.

The survival of the tarot and its perpetuation into the twenty-first century speaks to its ability to touch the very core of the human experience. Everything has changed—technology, society, transportation, social norms, infrastructure, architecture—and yet this set of images, by resonating with the timeless aspects of existence, has persevered. When using the tarot, you are tapping into a collective history, a cumulative usage. Even without the mention of magic or spirituality (though that will be mentioned here), it is hard to deny that you are touching upon something larger than yourself when working with the cards.

Most people I speak to about the work I do seem to understand that on some level, even the ones who claim that tarot is bullshit (more on those people later), because one of the first things I hear when I say I'm a tarot reader is, "Well, I don't want to know if anything bad is going to happen to me. Or my family or my boyfriend or dog or anyone I know." Which is fair. I wouldn't want to know any of that, either.

To be perfectly honest, something bad probably is going to happen to you or someone or something you care about at some point. That is the law of probability, not magic. There are ways to divine such unwelcome information, but the tarot, used with the intention of healing, doesn't predict future disaster. The tarot has a number of dark and difficult cards (I call them "shitty cards" for the sake of word economy, although they are among my favorites in the deck), the most universally dreaded one being Death. In all of the readings I've given, the Death card represented a literal death twice, and both times it was to the relief, not terror, of my client.

The large degree of skepticism with which I first met the tarot was quelled by the unflinching honesty of the cards. The tarot does not shy away from the jagged edges of existence. It is not some fluffy angel deck where every card is a positive affirmation, because that ain't life, fam. When you're totally on your game, you've worked your ass off and you're standing in a period of ease and enjoyment, the cards will reflect that. If you're offtrack, working a job that is murdering your soul or married to the wrong person, the cards will elucidate that, as well. If the cards could speak as a collective, I would imagine they would say something like, "We care about your life more than we care about your feelings." They are an energetic chiropractic session, and sometimes it hurts. But there is something distinctly satisfying about cracking things back into alignment. They will call you on your shit and maybe piss you off from time to time. They will not, however, predict your death. But you're probably still freaking out about this so there is a whole Shitty Cards section to further break this down (page 129).

The tarot is not meant for solely cognitive interpretation. The central fact of the tarot's existence is its imagery, and intellectual discernment alone will lead to freak-outs at the sight of the Death card because of our societally conditioned, pre-conceived notions of dying. The visuals are designed to surpass cognition and evoke a response. Pay attention to what feelings an image stirs in you, and try to ingest the cards visually and viscerally. It's an exercise that trains the mind to trust the process of our bodies, our guts, our hearts and our intuition. Eventually, the mind will accept when its faculties aren't needed, and it can rest. Regardless of what deck you use—and there are literally thousands to choose from—the images are its heart and soul.

Remember this: The cards will make themselves known to you. Remaining mysterious does not serve them or you. They want to be known.

Hundreds upon hundreds of readings have convinced me that the tarot can provide a person with clarity, insight and direction in absolutely any aspect of their life. Whether you're debating renewing the lease on your apartment or feeling unsure about your life's purpose. Big or small, mundane or metaphysical, the tarot can be used as an effective and powerful way of gathering information and laying out possible maps.

The tarot is made up of two parts—the Major and Minor Arcana. *Arcana* is defined as secrets or mysteries, and so it would follow that the Major Arcana contain the major mysteries of existence and the Minor Arcana, the minor ones.

The Major Arcana

The Major Arcana are the big dog, hot shit, major players of the tarot. Starting with The Fool, card zero, and ending in The World, card twenty-one, the Major Arcana capture the landmarks and lessons that a person experiences throughout a lifetime. They speak to the bigger, overarching energies that underpin the specific, day-to-day happenings. Hindsight allows us to look at a period of our life and extract the moral of a particular story, but we cannot always see why the fuck we need to go through this super shitty, difficult thing while it's happening. The Major Arcana reveal moments when we are standing at a pivotal point or there is a larger energy at play, hidden in the granular details.

The breakup that eviscerated you. Recovering from an addiction. Your mother dying. A spiritual awakening wherein you realized you needed to leave your job and move to another country. These are possible manifestations of the Major Arcana.

In addition to being the heaviest hitting, the Major Arcana also comprise the most iconic, famous and infamous cards in the deck. The Lovers, The Hermit, Death, The Devil and The Sun are among the more prominently featured and well known.

There is a natural progression to the Major Arcana's journey; a narrative unfolds as you make your way from The Fool toward The World. The story is fundamentally familiar because you are experiencing it right now. As you get to know the cards, you'll find yourself connecting your experiences to the archetypes. This is an empowering practice. It takes away the victim mentality that makes us ask, "Why is this happening to me," and replaces it with an understanding that all experiences, light and dark, are necessary for our development and are worthy of honoring.

The Minor Arcana

The Minor Arcana, always a bridesmaid, never a bride, serve to support and further clarify the Major Arcana's messages. If I pull six cards for a client and only one is Major Arcana, I will read the five Minor cards under the umbrella of the one Major. For example, if the Major Arcana card pulled is The Hanged Man, a card of surrender and detachment, the surrounding cards will point to areas of your life where you are being asked to let go.

Making up the remaining fifty-six cards of a tarot deck, the Minor Arcana represent situations, circumstances and people in our lives. Broken out in format almost exactly like a deck of playing cards, the Minor Arcana are set into four suits—Ace through Ten—and the court cards. In *The Way of the Tarot*, Alejandro Jodorowsky compares the four suits of the tarot to the four legs of a table upon which the tabletop of the Major Arcana rests.

Though the Minor Arcana do not inherently hold the same gravity as their Major counterparts, they are still formidable players. First of all, there are more of them, just as worldly details of life can feel more pressing than the cosmic soul lessons of it, no matter how woke you are. Say you have found your calling in the world to open an animal sanctuary (a shift that could be represented by Judgment), you still have a ton of Minor Arcana shit to do to get you there. Filing for non-profit status, hiring the right people, finding the perfect piece of land within your price range and probably spending some time plagued by the "Who the fuck am I?" question and taking measures to heal that in order to move forward—these are measures that the Minor cards will delineate.

Your shitty boss, creaky apartment you're dying to move out of, unreliable bank account and annoying roommate could all be represented by the Minor Arcana. And we all know that an annoying roommate can be all-consuming and life-ruining, even if it doesn't securely plug into your soul's mission in this universe. It could, however, be a force that pushes you into a new apartment, where one of your roommates is the future CFO of your animal sanctuary.

WHAT THE FUCK
IS MAGIC?

It is impossible to talk about the tarot and how it works without talking about magic, so let's just go ahead and get that out of the way right now.

This is when people are like, "Okay, but do you actually believe in magic?" Yes. I literally, completely believe in magic. I'm not talking about fantastical magic, though I am not ruling that out. Are there monks in a cave in Asia levitating their monk friends and LOLing? Maybe. Are there witch doctors in the swamps of the South resurrecting snakes? I wouldn't rule it out. But this isn't the magic that I'm talking about. The experiences of magic most detectable to us are signs and synchronicities served up by the universe. It is available to us always, but it is a matter of tweaking our perceptions to be capable of identifying when magic crosses our path. This process of expanding your awareness is a natural consequence of learning the tarot.

Occultists, magicians, healers and lightworkers wiser and more experienced than I have endeavored to answer this question, to articulate the largely intangible energy of magic in a way that others may understand. But magic cannot be understood unless it is experienced— it is trying to explain the hues of autumn to the colorblind. However, most people have come into contact with magic in their lives in some capacity, so to wrap our heads around it we need only identify moments it's been present.

At my mother's burial, a white moth landed on my black dress and stayed there for the duration of the service. My six year old brain made the connection that a white moth represented a visitation from my mother's spirit. Long after I shunned the idea of magic and entered a very dark decade and a half, I could not shake the association I made between her and white moths, and they appeared everywhere. The morning of my Bat Mitzvah, the first time I consumed a hallucinogen, as I was getting arrested in the parking lot of my high school, as I sat on my roof ten years after her death and read her suicide note for the first time, my high school *and* college graduations. Most of these appearances were met with frustration or anger, especially where she came as a reminder I was travelling down her same dangerous road of destruction and addiction. Reflecting on those instances, the anger was connected to belief. A reluctant one, one I had no interest in, but I never doubted that the moments the moth appeared, she was there as well.

Replace the word magic with whatever you want—spirit, universal intelligence, miracles, coincidence, luck, god. Replace it with the feeling that you get when you're thinking about someone and your song comes on the radio, or the sensation that occurs when you walk into at empty room and feel certain you're not alone. When you make it to the top of the mountain and look out into the distance and are reminded of how small and big you are at the same time. When you meet a perfect stranger and can't shake the feeling you know them. When you felt something would happen before it did. Replace this with those annoying clichés: "there are no mistakes" or "everything happens for a reason," which even the most magic-averse somehow get on board with. But that's magic, too.

In a more literal sense, magic is the manipulation of energies. While telekinesis or clairvoyance are extreme versions of this, there are simpler forms as well. It is a common belief in magic that energy follows intention. This is why mindful practices like building altars, meditation, journaling and rituals are integral to a magical life. The conscious cultivation of intention is a crucial beginning to establishing a relationship with the tarot.

It is magic that makes it possible to sit down with a complete stranger and pull cards that accurately and powerfully mirror their reality. There is a collective purpose created between the tarot, client and reader that is energetically absorbed and expressed through the cards.

One of the most commonly asked questions I get about the tarot is this: So how does it work? After much thought, I now simply answer by saying: magic.

I named my store Everyday Magic because a) it's a great name, isn't it? and b) it succinctly imparts my thoughts on the matter. Magic is not a theory. It is not just a striking sunset, or a synchronistic moment, or a perfect day. Magic is not a rarefied phenomenon nor does it serve us to treat it as such. There is magic in the tragedy, the shitty hair days, the excruciating pain, the arbitrary. There's magic in the hustle, in the success and the failure. Allow yourself to see magic in every square inch and your life changes. The light and goodness are as equally sacred as the dark and the muck. To live a magical life is not synonymous with living a flawless life, or even a righteous one. Rather, it is accepting, embracing and surrendering to all of it. To the beautiful mess of being a human with a body and also a soul.

Now, I truly believe everything is magic. I see it in my work, my friendships and my pain. It is magic because I don't believe, in all of its light and dark, that any of it is a mistake. Science knows that we have a beating heart, but what makes it beat? Why is it beating? Magic is leaning into the gorgeous mystery of it all.

Initially, I was reluctant to put words to the physical experience of magic because it feels impossible to do so without cheapening it is some way. But that is true of everything written about in this book. The words are simply a skeleton. Your experience, the amazing moments you will come to through the tarot, the identification of magic, a more aligned life, a distinct sense of ease are the muscle and blood and vital organs. The tarot, in all its magic, is just an object. We animate it with the intention we bring to the cards.

Alan Chapman writes in his book *Advanced Magick for Beginners,* "There are no laws unless you create them, there are no secrets unless you pretend. If magick is limited only by your imagination, just how beautiful will you make your magick, how ecstatic?"

I've grown accustomed to clients reaching out and saying, "You will never believe what happened," followed by a story of how magic worked in their life.

I assure you, I will believe it. It's not that I won't be awed by it or grateful for the reminder or delighted by the anecdote. But I now know magic to be real in the same way I know other, very uncomplicated facts.

There is no need for blind faith. Come to magic with your doubt, your skepticism, your fear, your preconceived notions. But come.

HOW THE FUCK DO I CHOOSE A DECK?

You may have picked up this book because you either bought or received a deck and don't know WTF to do with it. If you feel a connection to the deck you have, start there. If you don't have one, do not resonate with its imagery, or feel unsure about how to choose, let's hop to it. There are an overwhelming number of tarot decks available, with new ones being published all of the time. A simple Internet search will bring you to lists of thousands of decks with pictures and descriptions.

Start simple and find a deck that makes some kind of intuitive sense to you. The Rider-Waite tarot has survived the test of time and continues to be the most popular and widely used deck despite being over a century old. This is an excellent deck for beginners because of the narrative-based imagery and the plethora of websites and guidebooks corresponding to its imagery. There are more resources available to learn from if you choose a more established deck, but it is not essential. I learned from a modern indie deck whose images vary dramatically from its more traditional counterparts. Go for what you are drawn to, whether it be animals and nature, anime, Native American culture, Hinduism, Goddesses, steampunk, cooking, cats—if you're into it, there's probably a tarot deck for it.

If possible, find a shop near you that sells tarot cards and get your ass over there. Spend time with the decks, review the images, feel the weight of the paper. Finding your deck should feel something like Harry in Mr. Ollivander's wand shop when he finds his wand and red and gold sparks shoot out of the tip. I'm only mildly exaggerating. Finding a deck that resonates with you both etherically and aesthetically is a delicate alchemy.

There are indie decks that, because they are self-published, are not widely available and can't be found in most new age stores. In which case, the World Wide Web will have to do. These decks are often made by a single artist, however, and their makers can be easily reached for questions. The Fountain Tarot, Lumina Tarot, Spirit Speak Tarot, Starchild Tarot, Small Spells Tarot and Wooden Tarot are all stunning, resonant indie decks self-published by badass magic makers.

I don't believe it matters what deck you use. There are innumerable ways to effectively illustrate the tarot's archetypes. If using a more modern deck, I would make sure that the artist has experience with the tarot and did not create it solely out of aesthetic enthusiasm. More importantly, make sure it's actually a tarot deck. There is a set structure to the tarot— seventy-eight cards, twenty-two Major Arcana, etc. There are oracle decks that put tarot in their title and decks that follow the seventy-eight card model but bastardize the archetypes into oblivion. If it has four suits and doesn't re-name the Major Arcanas something unrecognizable from their original title, you're in the right place.

I also recommend choosing one deck and committing to it. You will be cultivating a relationship with these cards throughout the course of your experience. Like any relationship, intimacy and trust grow with time.

There is a superstition around buying your own tarot deck. Story goes that the deck intended for you will find you somehow in the form of a gift or inheritance. In my experience, this is not required for a deck to be yours and work for you. What matters is that you really, really like your cards, that you feel drawn to and curious about them. If, for whatever reason, you feel strongly about not buying your own deck, find another friend who also wants one and gift them to each other.

A Note on Fucking Gender

There are so many times, especially in the arena of magic, where language fails us. We tinker with it, bend it, expand it the best we can to capture the substance of what we're talking about. However, at the end of the day, we are attempting to fit the ethereal, spiritual, elusive and esoteric within the confines of words. It can be said that this is the struggle that all writers face, that we wrestle with language to generate something beautiful and truer and greater than the sum of its parts, but it feels especially pertinent to mention it here. As we begin the journey into the tarot's arcana, we will find that nearly all cards are gendered — gender, another construct that fails us. And yet . . .

We cannot fully understand the cards if we remove these associations. They are not in place to be divisive, or exclusive. It has nothing to do with gender identity or sexuality or genitals or politics. Rather, the gender of the cards speaks to their quintessential energies.

I will ask that, for the sake of honoring the integrity of the tarot's structure and archetypes, that you look at the concepts of feminine and masculine energy outside of the confines of physical gender and not disregard them altogether. Each person has within them a combination of masculine and feminine energy, and the tarot speaks to the reconciliation of these dualities to achieve balance and harmony within ourselves. There are cards that speak to the attainment of this balance—The Lovers, Justice, Temperance, Judgment—and then there are cards that are pure expressions of a singular energy. Most masculine energies have feminine counterparts, speaking to the incomplete nature of possessing just one of these traits. The Magician and The High Priestess, The Empress and The Emperor, The Moon and The Sun are all examples of the masculine and feminine completing each other.

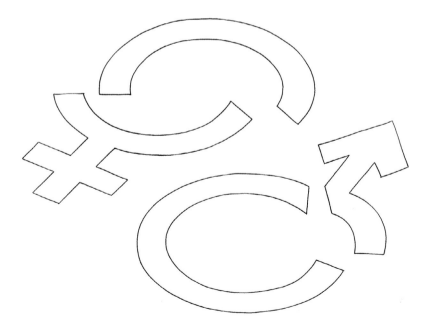

So, with that said, let's get clear on what characterizes these energies.

High Feminine Energy
- Receptive
- Intuitive
- Compassionate
- Passive/inactive
- Nurturing
- Emotional
- Wise
- Vulnerable

High Masculine Energy
- Assertive
- Active
- Rational
- Protective
- Decisive
- Confident
- Practical
- Strong

Low Feminine Energy
- Backstabbing
- Passive/aggressive
- Manipulative
- Victim
- Co-dependent

Low Masculine Energy
- Aggressive
- Violent
- Corrupt
- Controlling
- Unavailable

While the words fall short, I hope you can experience the soul of the sentiment beyond the language. I feel the same way when I work with words like love or god. You can call it yin and yang, light and dark, active and passive—what is important is that we do not ignore the truth of duality, as it is at the core of what makes the tarot such a powerful tool for self-study and reconciliation.

THE
MAJOR ARCANA

0—THE FOOL

The creation of something new is not accomplished by the intellect but by the play instinct acting from inner necessity. The creative mind plays with the objects it loves.
—Carl Jung

freedom / risk / impulse / trust / naïve / inner child / ignorance / adventure / joyful / child / journeyer / precipice / unhurt / ready / new soul / beginning / bursting / enthusiasm / unprepared / blind faith / ignition

Card Meaning

The Fool symbolizes the leap into incarnation. As card zero, he is an outlier of the Major Arcana, the beginning before the beginning. A sponge, a blank slate for the experiences laid out for him in the following cards. Possessing the energy of the newborn, The Fool is both cosmically connected—new enough to hold on to the memory of the divine oneness from which he came—and fearless—possessing no knowledge of the world he is about to step into and therefore too uninformed to be afraid.

Traditionally, The Fool is about to take a leap off a cliff. Most depictions include a warning symbol cautioning him against the leap, commonly in the form of a dog nipping at his feet. This warning does not come from us. It is not our intuition or inner voice. It is the collective warning of societal programming, learned fear and deeply ingrained self-doubt. Embodying the energy of The Fool is an act of self-trust so radical that it allows us to take risks that may seem crazy to others. When we align with The Fool, we do not doubt ourselves, even if it feels like we should. He invites us to set aside our pride and everything we think we know in exchange for the possibility of a new beginning. However, this is not always appropriate action. The question we must consider upon meeting The Fool is when does it serve us to go into a situation unbiased and when is it wiser to make decisions based on our experience. While The

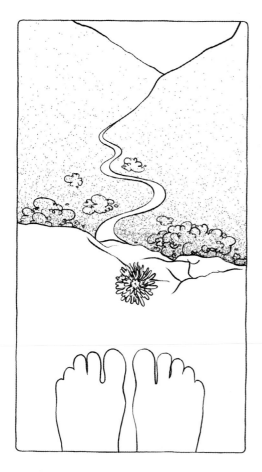

Fool has many merits, he is entirely devoid of wisdom, and therefore his fearlessness can put him in danger if employed in the wrong circumstances.

In my experience, The Fool represents a risk worth taking. Symbolizing pre-creation and cosmic consciousness, he awakens our spiritual memory and prepares us for new opportunity. We are likely to surprise ourselves here. So used to using our ego as a compass, The Fool activates a completely different navigation system. Every cell in our body longs for this unexpected journey for which we have no road map and no destination. Our bones are buzzing with purpose that we cannot fathom with our mind or articulate with our ego. And yet, we must jump. To defy this instinct is to deny life itself.

There are hints, feelings and inclinations this next step is right, but nothing quantifiable. This is why The Fool has historically represented madness and insanity, because his choice defies logic and reason. He is total impulse, pure spontaneity, eternally leaping into the present moment.

Anecdote

Quitting my job wasn't what grown-ups would call a "good idea." I'd been working for a little over a year and got a promotion a few months before I received my tarot deck. I had a sure thing, a steady paycheck, coworkers I loved, a boss I respected, health insurance and the emotional security essential to an early-twenties recent-grad who was totally freaked out about whether or not I could ever successfully adult.

When I gave my two weeks' notice, I had two hundred dollars in my bank account and absolutely zero idea of what came next. But I had to jump. It wasn't an option. In all honesty, it took about an hour of owning a tarot deck to know that this would take me in new and unexpected directions, that the job I worked so hard to get instantly became a dream belonging to some former version of me. It was the craziest thing I've ever done, and the best decision I've ever made.

In a Reading

The Fool often shows up as an opportunity for a major new beginning that requires taking a leap, or a risk. An upcoming birth or fertile ground for new creative endeavors. It could symbolize a move, a career change or unexpectedly falling in love. An urging to stop taking yourself so seriously, to avoid getting bogged down by details, preconceived notions or fear. Look at a situation with fresh eyes. Listen to your gut. Be open to a new experience, or to being surprised. Consider always the positioning of The Fool—what direction is he facing? What card is he leaping into? What position is he in in the greater context of the spread? If surrounded by ominous cards, it may be a warning that now is not the best time to take a leap, or imply naivety or ignorance to the pitfalls of a situation. The Fool encourages spontaneous and impulsive action over rational planning.

1—THE MAGICIAN

It's handled.
—Olivia Pope

power / manifestation / genius / willpower / mapmaker / creation / master / resources / god-force / action / boss / poised / prepared / expert / self-reliance / elemental / leader / self-assured / fast

Card Meaning

In high school, my creative writing teacher took a small group of students to hear one of my favorite poets give a lecture. I was an angsty teenager and indifferent to pretty much everything, with writing being one of the few exceptions. I listened, enthralled, to this man compare the experience of reading a good poem to that of standing inside a grand cathedral. With every aspect of the architecture meant to inspire awe in its occupants, it is a testament to structure allowing the understanding of space. We are always surrounded by infinite space, but inside this expansive cathedral, looking up at the high, vaulted ceilings, we can actually feel it. An ethereal concept becomes, in that moment, a tangible presence.

This is the energy of The Magician. He is the creative force, the manifestation current, the god energy, the resources that facilitate an experience. He is always present, but this card speaks to an acute awareness of this powerful archetype.

The Magician asks us to contemplate the value of using tricks in service of the Higher Self. A Shaman does a healing on a person, detects a blockage somewhere in their body and energetically removes it. At the same time, they use a sleight of hand to make it appear to the person that a small rock or pebble has been physically pulled from that area of their body. The Magician toes the line between the true miracle-worker and the trickster, just as the cathedral manipulates our senses into being aware of a grandness that is ever-present but often overlooked. With this in mind, when getting to know this card we must also

contemplate the difference between experiencing The Magician (standing inside the architecture) and being The Magician (being the architect).

When this energy is embodied in an individual, please call me because you found my future husband. He exudes confidence and skillfulness in all he does, with complete control over his many faculties. With the entire Minor Arcana at his disposal, it seems like he is capable of anything. He can build a cabin in the woods or manage a hedge fund, be a stay-at-home-dad or CEO. With full access to his masculinity and femininity, emotionality and practicality, command and surrender, wisdom and wonder, he's taken the best qualities of the Minor cards and distilled them into a cogent singularity. Because of his vast resources, he possesses a distinct ability to make things possible for other people. Whatever problem you bring to him, he always seems to know a guy or have the specific wrench you need to fix that leaky faucet. His capacity for empathy is great and his ability to identify a person's needs is effortless. You're all invited to the wedding.

When we experience The Magician, the risk of The Fool has paid off. We took the leap and landed on solid ground, and now it is time to take action. The Magician is traditionally depicted with all of the symbols of the Minor Arcana because in many ways he is the dispenser of them. The tools are on the table for you, you will be given what you need when you need it, but the action is yours to take. People who are in the energy of The Magician are hustling, maybe stressed, very busy and making shit happen. It's a period of rapid-fire, nearly hysterical receiving. Doors are opening all around you, opportunities are presenting themselves, your goals are being activated and made possible. In The Fool, we say yes to the universe and in The Magician the universe says yes back to us.

Anecdote

The week I quit my job I basically walked around in a state of sheer terror. The first day, I walked into a shop wearing a shirt with a tarot symbol on it and the woman working there asked me about it. When I told her I read tarot, she immediately invited me to work at an event there that weekend. Those first few days, I made twice as much giving readings as I would have working my old job. Every week I expected to fall on my face, and every week my schedule filled. By word of mouth (and magic) my practice grew in ways I never could have fathomed or planned for. Within the first few months, the tarot took me to Brooklyn basement parties, Upper East Side penthouse baby showers, upstate wedding receptions, non-profit galas and, once, to a very open-minded church. I worked with clients in Australia, Kenya, London, Chile, Iceland and Vietnam. I was contacted for interviews, documentaries, podcasts and—at the risk of sounding too meta—book deals.

Most of the time it felt like I was running alongside something growing beyond my control. I was exhausted, exhilarated, overwhelmed and very, very busy. My social life also disappeared, I repeatedly crossed my own boundaries, my self-care was garbage and both my boyfriend and my dog experienced unprecedented neglect. But there wasn't time to appreciate the success, let alone consider the consequences. My dream was coming true, and I was being invited deeper and deeper into its manifestation. It was all I could do to pick my jaw up off the floor and continue saying yes to the opportunities coming my way. And yet, through the surprise and delight and gratitude, there was something else. A knowing. A bone-level understanding that I had clicked into something that was right beyond what I could comprehend at the time. I felt more competent, more capable of embracing this expansion than I had ever felt of anything else in my life. I felt myself working with The Magician as much as he was working for me. All my energy, every resource I had, went to keeping up with this wild ride.

In a Reading
It is time for action, most likely of the rapid-fire, borderline-batshit variety. Buckle up and get ready to work. The Magician engulfs us in an intense creative energy, everything we want is available to us in this space. Utilize both your skills and the resources at your disposal to achieve success. He points to the efficacy of intention-setting and shows us our ability to manifest. The Magician lends itself to feeling competent and capable. When considering if something is a good idea, or has the fruitful potential, The Magician answers "fuck yes." This highly charged energy tells us it's time to fully focus and commit to whatever it is we're trying to get done. Act now, breathe later. It's worth it to hustle during this time. The Magician is also a very magical man, and can present itself as a powerful romantic equal to The High Priestess.

2—THE HIGH PRIESTESS
The only real valuable thing is intuition.
—Albert Einstein

depth / mystery / receptive / ethereal / top bitch / self-trust / devotion / watchful / pure / still / goddess / arcana / ancient / intuitive / divine feminine

Card Meaning

The High Priestess is the ultimate initiator into the mysteries, embodying the ancient knowing that lives within us all. She comprises the feminine side of the tarot's astral power couple. If The Magician is the god, she is the goddess. If he is religion, she is mysticism. Where he is active and vocal, she is passive and silent. And yet, they are entirely equal in their power. She is devoted to aligning herself with the divine, plumbing its mysteries and knowing it personally. Beyond passion, emotion, sexuality and humanity, The High Priestess represents total purity of spiritual intention.

Because The High Priestess is a disembodied energy, she takes us outside of the baser desires that accompany being human. In a life that is constantly buzzing, that interrupts stillness at every turn, that is full of toxins and indulgences, we commune with The High Priestess when we are longing to detox and know ourselves. In a society that doesn't acknowledge the legitimacy of feminine power, here we are reminded. She is accessed through meditation, in quiet moments. We cannot be fully informed human beings in the world without knowing ourselves in this way first. Without the depth of The High Priestess, the message of The Magician is vapid, and he is more trickster than truth. We can receive the tools and act upon them, but until we internalize that action and make our own meaning out of it, we are not woke. Any kind of spiritual, channeling or creative work requires that we have access to this consciousness. It could be said that The Magician facilitates the recognition of divine energy, whereas The High Priestess allows for the experience of it and entrance into it.

When you know something is true, on a gut level, beyond a shadow of a doubt, but don't know how you know it, you are tuning in to the wisdom of The High Priestess. We develop a relationship with her by trusting ourselves. It's the feeling we get when we know someone is lying, or sense familiarity in a stranger. When we doubt our intuition, when we dismiss a feeling as crazy, when we invalidate our instincts, we sever ourselves from the power she offers us.

The High Priestess doesn't give a fuck that she values intuition over intellect because she knows her intuition will never lead her astray. She speaks slowly and quietly, chews her food before swallowing it and radiates certainty even in her stillness. She's besties with the divine and relies on that unfailing connection for her power, which makes her unwaveringly powerful.

Anecdote

I met Milos a few months after I got sober. I was eighteen years old, college-bound and happy to be alive for the first time in my life. I was going to twelve-step meetings every night, having found a community there that felt like family and a program that freed me from the chains of addiction. Milos walked into the meeting, and I fell in love with him on sight. He was sporting a Jim Morrison shirt and the bluest eyes I've ever seen. When he shared his story, I heard my own truth in his words.

That night, he joined us at a friend's house, and we spent the night in her backyard, feet in the pool, talking until sunrise. It marked the beginning of the most magical summer of my life. In those short months, it felt like we sank through the crust of the earth, into its white-hot core. We electrified each other. We caught on fire and burned and burned and burned.

Milos and I spent a summer pushing each other into pools fully clothed with expensive watches on and cell phones in our pockets. Barefoot, burning incense on the beach. We called each other at all hours of the night with ideas for poetry and music and revolution. We bought journals and filled them with prose and innovations and plans. We filled our trunks with seashells and water bottles. We lay on the floors of bookstores and studied god. We deemed the song of the summer "Sugar Magnolia" by the Grateful Dead and called each other in the morning singing.

Summer slid between our fingers and toes, became tangled in our hair and stuck to the back of our calves. We clung onto it long after the last grains of sand swirled down our shower drains. The night before I left for Boston, I told him I wasn't going. I was going to postpone school and find a way to transfer to a school in Chicago. He was never more serious when he said that if I did that, he would never forgive me. He said I was ready. That I needed to go to school and I needed to write.

The next morning, I received a message from him as the airplane was taxiing out of the gate.

"I just want you to know how happy I am to have met you when I did. You have been a huge part of my recovery and I think the world of you. It won't be too long until I see you, but be the smart chick I know you are. You really are a sunshine daydream."

As I read it, I became aware of a feeling I had had for months, living right under the surface of my awareness. It was one that I couldn't articulate or grasp, but it motivated me all summer—to live as fully as I could, to cherish every moment, to write everything down so I wouldn't forget. The knowing materialized, as the plane took off, that I would never see Milos again.

I landed to the news of his death. A hiking accident. He was leaning over a cliff to gaze at the view and fell eighty feet.

I've since retraced my steps and familiarized myself with the knowing, the intuitive hints that I was living in something precious and ethereal. More than that, I identified the sense I had all along that it was worth remembering, documenting, letting in fully and without doubt. I recognized in him a teacher and a soul mate and a brother, and the force of that connection along with the understanding of its transience allowed for it to fix my chemistry, uncross my wires, change me on a cellular level beyond anything I'd experienced before it. Not a day has passed since where I have not felt him with me.

In a Reading

This card calls for non-action. Get still within yourself and connect with your own wisdom. The High Priestess heightens our awareness of secret or hidden information. She also comes through in dreams to deliver intuitive messages. It may be time to develop a meditation practice, rekindle your spirituality or sharpen your psychic abilities. Draw to the esoteric, etheric and occult. Trust your intuition. You don't need the advice of other people. You already know what's true. Give yourself permission to make emotional decisions. Maybe you've let yourself become too tangled up in or influenced by external energies. She calls for simplicity—to withdraw from involvement and return to ourselves.

3—THE EMPRESS

I have always been the woman of my dreams
—Nayyirah Waheed

overflowing / abundance / feminine / passion / nurturing / lush / indulgent / sensual / seductive / embodied / welcoming / beauty / queen / fertile / maternal / generative / confidence / richness / unashamed

Card Meaning

The Empress is the first embodied energy in the Major Arcana, and therefore represents the birth of the physical world. Her capacity for creation is vast, and she encompasses the humanity and passion conspicuously lacking in The High Priestess. As they say, find you a girl who can do both. The High Priestess and Empress together comprise the full force of feminine energy.

First and foremost, The Empress is the mother. Her maternal instinct is fierce and she will literally fuck you up if you mess with what she loves. Think Molly Weasley taking out Bellatrix Lestrange in the final battle of Hogwarts. With that said, her love is boundless and extends to all who wish to bask in her warmth. There is nothing that she cannot find beauty in, and people are naturally drawn to this nurturing energy. You can tell her the worst thing

you've ever done, the things you are most ashamed of, the things about you that you find ugly and she will, by some love-induced alchemy completely unique to her, transmute it into something magnificent. It is an ability that comes from self-love and acceptance. Her makeup is flawless, her home is open and welcoming and she wants to feed you and listen to you talk about boys.

In addition to being a maternal energy, The Empress is also an inherently sensual one. When you walk into a room feeling and looking fierce, you're channeling your girl. When you throw a dinner party that is on point down to flower arrangements and decorative napkins, The Empress is pouring herself a glass of vino. When you decide to blow off work to lay on your couch in a face mask with a box of pizza resting on your stomach, she's drafting the fake sick e-mail to the office.

A deeply (and sometimes stubbornly) emotional archetype, she acts from a place of feeling and can be reactionary and irresponsible as a result. This hot energy is subdued by the austerity of the High Priestess and then grounded and made viable by her man The Emperor. The High Priestess gives us the space to learn about our gifts and The Empress is the beginning of bringing them to life and offering them to the world. She is masterful at self-care and she knows her body to be beautiful.

The Empress is never depleted because she knows how to accept love as well as give it. The crucial flaw we make as mere humans and not perfect tarot archetypes is that many of us are skilled at nurturing and offering care to others but do not know how to absorb it when it is offered to us. Her constant creative output is fueled by love, and her identity is informed by her creativity and the products of her creation. If feeling uninspired or blocked, her energy is a robust tonic.

Anecdote

Last night I was lying in bed with my two best friends. We weren't doing anything particularly noteworthy; folding laundry, eating pizza, playing music, showing each other dumb stuff on our phones. We were laughing. We were doing face masks. We were tangled up in a human pretzel situation without really being aware of who was touching whom. I have absolutely zero secrets from these two girls, and the sense of comfort, well-being and connection I feel in their presence is so effortless that it has become second nature. It is only when I step back that I can appreciate how extraordinary it is and how empty my life would be without it. There's not a thing they could say or do that would make me think less of them. There's not a thing I have that I wouldn't give them. There's not a single blessing in this life that I do not believe they are completely deserving of. My friend's fiancé came home and found us all there, confused because she backed out of a dinner earlier saying she needed a night in alone to recharge. She was being honest. The Empress is the creator of the cozy, nourishing, unworried love you feel for the people you can be with and be alone at the same time.

In a Reading

The Empress shows up as a resurgence of creativity and passion. The act of creating something out of love. A situation may call for femininity—whether it is vulnerability, softness, nurturing or emotionality. Be gentle. Be generous with the care you give to yourself and others. Look for the beauty in all things. Be forgiving of your humanity. A symbol of motherhood, fertility and birth. A warm, maternal figure. Give yourself permission to be rich and abundant, even decadent. Seeing your body as beautiful. Acceptance of sexuality and sensuality. Like The High Priestess, she makes decisions from an emotional place, but doesn't have the same sharp intuition as her more reserved counterpart, so The Empress can also be an indication of hot-headedness or being overly-emotional.

4—THE EMPEROR

Leadership is about submission to duty, not elevation to power.
—Gordon Tootoosis

authority / steadfast / father / consistent / deliberate / structure / balanced / rigid / reliable / safety / power / contained / logical / leader / self-possessed / grounded / proprietor / security / fixed / productive / objective

Card Meaning

The Emperor brings order, structure and organization into the world. A triggering card for many for its connection to society, authority and power; accurately interpreting The Emperor depends upon understanding him in his intended energy and then discerning if it has been twisted in some way. Think about the intent of implementing a police force in our society versus the present day reality of it. The duty of leadership is a great one, and the task undertaken by The Emperor is not without sacrifice.

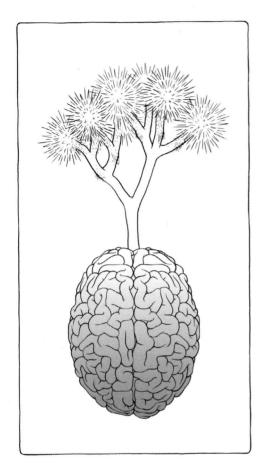

When The Emperor is doing his job well, you don't notice him. He stepped into this position of power to be of service to others. The holder of space and representative of institutions that bring order and balance, he works tirelessly and transparently so that others can feel safe. In its purest form, The Emperor's rule is ego-less, coming from a place of loving responsibility and an understanding of the importance of healthy structure. Without this integrity, corruption invariably ensues.

The Emperor gets a bad rap, often written off as a square or an asshole. The Empress is boundless, flowing creativity. Her edges are liquid. She is inspiration itself. But we all know someone who has gorgeous creative potential but does not know what to do with it. Unexpressed creativity will inevitably turn into a destructive force. The Emperor harnesses the creativity of The Empress and gives it boundaries, definition and purpose. This is the natural function of masculine structure: to maintain order so that others may succeed inside of it.

Say you are an artist and you channel your Empress energy to make your work. Without The Emperor, that art sits in the room it was created in. We channel his energy to price our pieces, coordinate with galleries to show it, answer e-mails, schedule appointments, manage our social media and generally slay the hustle. This is how they are the perfect earthly power couple. Without The Emperor, the ripeness of The Empress rots on the vine. Without The Empress, The Emperor is bloodless and boring.

How does structure allow for freedom? Can we feel freedom without structure? One of the most perfect earthly structures is that of a twelve-step recovery program. Intended for addictions of all sorts, rigorously working the steps of this program permits a freedom from addiction.

The Emperor holds this consistent, objective, productive structure for all. If correctly implemented, they mirror the natural laws of the universe—harmonious when followed and chaotic when broken.

Anecdote

I fell in love with my dog Zadie the second I walked into the animal shelter and saw her. She was skin and bones, had missing teeth and a wrecked digestive system and displayed telltale signs of abuse. When they took her out of her crate she literally jumped into my arms, and I hugged her and wept and promised that nothing bad would ever happen to her again. We bonded intensely and instantly. She followed me around my apartment, cried when I went into another room and suffered from severe separation anxiety.

Dogs are happiest when they do not have to think for themselves, at their most relaxed when there is a set time to eat, play, go out and sleep. The structure fosters a sense of safety, and the consistency builds trust with their caretaker. Training Zadie was one of the hardest things I ever did. I leashed her in a corner of the apartment and largely ignored her for parts of the day so she could see that if I walked out of sight, I'd eventually come back. After trying several methods with a trainer, it took using an electric collar to condition her out of screaming whenever I left the house. I cried through a lot of this. All I wanted to do was mush our faces together and never leave her side, but more than that I wanted her to be the happiest, healthiest dog she could be. Because this was my primary motivation, the implementation of discipline and the exertion of dominance were acts of love. It was emotionally trying and stretched my understanding of what it meant to love someone and how that love can be expressed. It showed me a way of being of service to another's well-being in a distinctly masculine capacity.

In a Reading

Opportunity for leadership. Time to get your shit together and get organized. Answer your e-mails, file your paperwork, dot your I's and cross your T's. A grounding, stabilizing force. A father or paternal figure. Implementing structure and organization. Employing logic and rationality to solve a problem. Working within pre-existing structures to see success. Being a boss. Offering security and comfort to others by directing or managing them. Professionally it could symbolize a promotion at work or taking on more responsibility. As an external force it can speak to coming into contact with officials, law enforcement and societal structures. The romantic match of The Empress.

5—THE HIEROPHANT

*Guru is not the goal. Anyone who establishes himself as a guru to be worshipped is
not a guru. Guru is like a boat for crossing the river. It is important to have a good boat,
and it is very dangerous to have a boat that is leaking. The boat brings you across the river.
When the river is crossed the boat is no longer necessary. You don't hang onto the boat
after completing the journey, and you certainly don't worship the boat.*
—Swami Rama of the Himalayas

gatekeeper / tradition / medium / catalyst / religion / community / channel /
teacher / conduit / priest / knowledge / communion / guide / axis /
shrouded / secrets / culture / convention

Card Meaning

The Hierophant comes into our lives in the form of a leader, teacher or mentor, particularly
in a spiritual capacity. Traditionally depicted as a religious figure and used interchangeably
with the title "The Pope," he has come to mean conventional religious customs and values.
However, there is a more expansive and inclusive definition of this sometimes polarizing
figure. The primary purpose of The Hierophant is to serve as a conduit between heaven and
earth. In that respect, each card in the tarot can be considered a Hierophant. Any person,
place, object or community from which we receive guidance or meaning, or connect to a
feeling of tribe, can be aligned with this archetype.

Who are our mentors? Whom do we entrust with our growth? The divine works through
us on earth, and it is essential to rely on others to progress on our paths. However, we would
be remiss if we forget that no matter how wise or spiritually connected someone is, they are
also human and therefore fallible. The true mentors want their students to outgrow them.
When agreeing to act as a guide to others, The Hierophant accepts the responsibility to do so
with integrity, selflessness and humility. They are channeling the divine but they are not god.
This is a tall order and a profound balancing act, as we are all humans with egos. I've taught
tarot to students who have gone on to see great success as professional readers. Alongside
my happiness for them and gratitude for the tarot's perpetuation have been twinges of
competition and fear. Again, The Hierophant is human, but to submit to these lower-self
impulses, to the illusion of lack and scarcity or to the myth of our own specialness puts your
humanity in opposition to your divinity. The ongoing challenge of The Hierophant is to keep
these sometimes competing energies in harmonious alignment. Failing to do so produces cult
leaders, corrupt religious figures and spiritual mediums who withhold or delay information
for their own gain.

And yet, with all of the possible downfalls of The Hierophant, we have a non-negotiable need for community in spiritual work. It is too hard, too lonely, too weird to go it alone. There is a time and place for solitary study, but when The Hierophant appears it is a sign that we need others around us and guidance we trust in order to progress. Whether it is a congregation, coven or therapy group, part of the human experience is relying on others to reflect our goodness—and divinity—back to us.

The Hierophant brings to the forefront the concept of spiritual authority. Who has it, and how is it claimed? In an era where people are rejecting the dogma of organized religion in droves in search of a more personal connection to their spirituality, the training of the Priest or the Rabbi is no longer the only way to identify a Hierophant. Every time I read for a client, they give me spiritual authority. When I go see a healer for bodywork, or a therapist for guidance, I hand them spiritual authority. The act of giving and receiving this should be a conscientious and consensual process. Hold it responsibly, and bestow it wisely.

Anecdote

The woman who gifted me my first tarot deck is, to this day, the greatest spiritual mentor and teacher I've ever had. She was my therapist at the time, and I felt like I owed her the world. Every miraculous thing that happened to me as a result of reading tarot I attributed to her. And, while she is definitely a goddess, I deified her into an idea and put her on a pedestal so high I could no longer see her. When she tried to explain she felt guided to give me the cards because she sensed a gift I already had, I didn't want to hear it. It was a well-intended but selfish mind-set. I wanted someone to worship. I wanted to credit an external source to help make sense of what was going on.

We eventually had a disagreement that turned into a significant fight. I was wrecked. While I was certain that I had cause for being upset, I was also struggling with the idea of her being wrong about something. When we came together and resolved, she apologized for her part and explained her reaction. In so doing, she became a human being with flaws and a past, capable of miscommunication and mistakes just like anyone else. I finally understood what she had been trying to tell me. The divine can act through a person, but it does not make them a god, or absolve them of their humanity. As I got up to leave, she smiled at me and said, "And now we can finally be equals in this work." I felt grateful that she saw me that way and also scared of shifting the power dynamic I'd grown accustomed to. Now, I see it with some of my clients who think I am an all-knowing source of psychic content when really I'm just eating Cheetos on my couch watching *Broad City*.

In a Reading

Most commonly, when The Hierophant shows up in a reading it is a sign to seek guidance. Whether it is a therapist, teacher, mentor, healer or community, your own resources will not suffice. To move forward, you must reach out. Someone has something that you need. Studying, learning, quenching spiritual curiosity. Belonging to a group, or finding your tribe. Negotiating the role of religion in your life, or questioning your religious upbringing. Can mean connecting with tradition and ritual, but can also point to following convention or falling into line. Finding your own way to spirituality. Remain mindful of whose counsel you keep and who you give spiritual authority to.

6—THE LOVERS

Believe in a love that is being stored up for you like an inheritance, and have faith that in this love there is a strength and a blessing so large that you can travel as far as you wish without having to step outside it.
—Rainer Maria Rilke, *Letters to a Young Poet*

union / completion / generosity / choice / equals / ease / radiance / connection / bliss / supported / intimacy / alignment / harmony / travel / ambivalence

Card Meaning

A welcome sight in any reading, The Lovers symbolize true partnership. It can be said that it is the marriage of The Empress and The Emperor by The Hierophant, the feminine and masculine elevating together and uniting in spiritual union. Together, these dualities equal something greater than the sum of their parts. United by mutual respect, common ground and clear communication, these partners amplify each other's strengths. They are both freer and better equipped to handle life's challenges because of their relationship to each other.

They found home in what they have created together and are fuller, stronger individuals because of it. Too often The Lovers is immediately associated with romance, but it is truly a card of intimacy.

The Lovers is a discovery of self through connection with others. There is a youthful quality to this card: It is near the beginning of the Major cards and comes before any of the shitty ones or figuring-out-who-you-are ones. There is a time and place for that. Here, we find relationships that mirror us, and in its reflection we gain clarity, or perhaps discover something entirely new.

Union as a fundamental ingredient to freedom is a central theme of The Lovers card, which offers food for thought on relationships with others as well as ourselves. While The Lovers does not address the heavy-hitting matter of destroying duality altogether, it does show the masculine and feminine uplifting and reciprocating each other as equals. Within an individual, this looks like unlocking full access to both our Emperor and Empress energies, and the ability to call upon either or both if needed. We are no longer at odds with competing aspects of ourselves. Now that you're not blocking your own shot, where will you go? Because duality is at play here, The Lovers can also represent choice.

Water seeks its own level, always, and we will not find this balance with another until we know it within ourselves. Yes, that is an overused-advice-column-shitty-annoying cliché. But it is also the magical principle, "As above, so below." Ask yourself this, what would a relationship look like if you were with someone who loved you exactly as much as you love yourself? If it directly reflects the amount of respect, consideration and intimacy you have with yourself, would you be satisfied? If your answer is sometimes, you're in good shape. The Lovers is an ideal, and no individual or couple lives in this euphoric energy at all times.

We do not have to be perfect, finished products to find love with another person. We do, however, need to not be at war with ourselves and to have a relationship with love not contingent on the other. This doesn't mean we always live in a pure, unadulterated state of self-love. There are still days where you feel disgusting because you ate pizza five days in a row, periods where you're not happy with an aspect of your life, or with life in general. But for the most part you think you're all right. You've experienced freedom, selflessness, surrender and fearlessness in love, so you know what The Lovers feels like. You'd probably date you.

If my experience as a tarot reader has taught me anything it's that life is hard, family is hard, work is hard, but relationships are the hardest. We fight for and with love in a way that is distinctly unique. It is essential. We cannot survive without it.

Anecdote

My best friend and her boyfriend had been dating for less than a year when they decided to move across the country together. She's an LA native, and while I tried my damndest to persuade her to move East over the course of our friendship, it was always met with a steadfast declaration that she would never leave California.

North Carolina is a place that neither of them knew, but when her boyfriend told her he was offered a job there, her immediate response was "we're going." Out of all the reactions she could have had in that moment—worrying about leaving her lifelong home, jumping to logistics, fear of an unknown place, wondering what the fuck she would do in this new city—her most immediate one was that they, as a unit, were going. In the short time she'd been with this person, a shift occurred. Everything she thought she could never live without in LA no longer seemed as urgent, or as right, as going. Her considerations had evolved from personal interests to a collective well-being—a paradigm shift of *me* to *we*—where they, as a unit, would be happiest. When she called me to tell me about the move, I was absolutely shocked, but didn't for a minute doubt the rightness of her decision. She stated it as a fact. There was no fear in her voice. She's an extremely family oriented person, and it was clear that in this relationship she had found the same feeling of home.

Five years later, they're still in North Carolina, married and the most disgustingly in love couple I have ever had the pleasure of knowing.

In a Reading

Travel, freedom, deciding between two options. Good omen for romantic relationships. True, balanced partnership. Union of dualities. Balancing masculine and feminine energies. Two people who perfectly complement each other. Getting out of your own way—the ability to go where you want and do what you want. Feeling protected by the love around you. Mutual respect. Two equals coming together. Satisfaction and contentment. Young love. Developing our own belief system through making choices. Intimacy, attraction and sexuality. Clearly and honestly communicating with others.

7—THE CHARIOT

I see it, I want it, I stunt, yeah, yellow bone it
I dream it, I work hard
I grind 'til I own it [...]
Sometimes I go off, I go off
I go hard, I go hard
Get what's mine, take what's mine,
I'm a star, I'm a star
Cause I slay, slay
I slay, hey, I slay, I slay
All day
—Beyoncé, *Formation*

drive / transition / execution / willpower / perseverance / progress /
movement / adolescence / exertion / independence / velocity / determination /
triumphant / naïve / brave / propulsion / focused / unstoppable

Card Meaning

If The Lovers represents the moment that we are not standing in our own way anymore, that we are truly free to go, then The Chariot represents going. Embodying rapid movement fueled by willpower, The Chariot shows us the mountains we can move when we are determined to get shit done. Unwilling to take no for an answer and singular in his purpose, there is no universe in which he can picture not accomplishing his goal.

If the first seven cards of the Major Arcana are reconciling society, the second seven reconciling ourselves and the third seven reconciling our spirituality and purpose—The Chariot, the last card of the first row, is standing on a precipice. We leave home, whatever that might mean, to go and find our own way.

I think of The Chariot as a kid going off to college: he's determined, he's passionate, he's ready to claim his space in the world. But he's also broke and doesn't know how to do his laundry or cook without a microwave. The Chariot is our first glimpse of independence and adult life. We're juvenile, we're dumb, but we're also motivated and in it to win it.

The Chariot's got some knight-in-shining-armor-vibes going for him, but he's also immature. In a romantic capacity this card can represent something that, while it may be fun and intense, doesn't have the longest shelf life. You know that person you met and were so in love with that within the first forty-eight hours you already planned a move, your future house's window treatments and children's names? That is the energy The Chariot sweeps us up in. When we start a ten-page paper the night before it's due and power through it using a combination of caffeine, desperation and Wikipedia, we're channeling our inner Chariot. When working to accomplish a goal and wired with adrenaline, you have harnessed this archetype. You don't need food. You ain't got time for sleep. The Chariot signifies an effort,

but it is an effort you want to make. When we align with this energy we are entirely present because the situation calls for our full attention.

An overtly masculine archetype, the tax of The Chariot is collected in the form of a huge energy expenditure. For this reason, be careful to not stay in it for too long. It takes a toll on the body, enables the workaholic and threatens burnout. It is jet fuel in a lawnmower engine. Use sparingly for triumph and success.

Anecdote

One summer while I was in college, I accepted an education and advocacy internship at a farm animal sanctuary in upstate New York. Near the end of my time there, I was sent to Ohio to gather signatures for a ballot initiative that was in desperate need of some last minute volunteers. Spearheaded by a coalition of animal rights organizations, the initiative implemented some very basic but much-needed welfare reform for farm animals in the state.

My supervisor told me to pack for a weekend and sent me to Columbus. In many of the counties we worked in, the main streets were ghost towns, and we needed to find people. We spent days outside of public libraries, hiding in Wal-Mart parking lots, making deals with gas station owners to approach their patrons, going door to door in trailer parks and subdivisions, sussing out registered voters and talking to them about farm animal rights—mostly in rural areas. We were heckled by farmers, threatened by police and kicked out of more places that I can count. Every morning the volunteers gathered at sunrise and called it quits somewhere around 11 p.m. Each day was met with gruelingly hot temperatures, canvassing miles in the one pair of flip-flops I had. But there was no fucking way we weren't going to get enough signatures on my watch. I stayed past the weekend and for the remaining two weeks until the deadline. I washed my two outfits with shampoo in the bathroom sink of my motel room. We worked fifteen-hour days for over two weeks straight. I've never worked so hard in my life, but I've also never felt more energized, focused or purposeful. We got the initiative on the ballot. When I returned to upstate New York, I slept for three consecutive days.

In a Reading

A massive effort or exertion of energy. Exercising your will you achieve what you want. Steadfast determination. Not taking no for an answer. Singularity of focus. Quick action. Travel and movement. Goal oriented. Obsessiveness. Stubbornness. Graduation from adolescence into adulthood. Building self-confidence through accomplishing goals. Taking the reins in a situation. Feeling your leadership and the power of ego. Dominating something.

8—STRENGTH

Every desire of your body is holy;
Every desire of your body is
Holy.
—Hafiz

sexuality / alignment / grace / soothe / restraint / maturation / integration / softness / feminine power / cooperation / self-mastery / dominion / taming / primal / renewal / submission / instincts / compassion / influence

Card Meaning

Where The Chariot is the implementation of masculine force, Strength is an expression of feminine power. There is a marked sense of maturity, deliberation and self-awareness present in Strength, who took the wildfire energy of The Chariot and internalized it into a more viable slow burn.

In traditional tarot decks, the Strength card depicts a woman holding open a lion's mouth with her hands. This is not a display of physical fortitude. She has not overpowered the lion. Rather, she trained it and earned its trust. There is a wisdom and utility in her choice of handling this wild animal that ultimately serves them both. If the lion is our primal nature and inherent wildness, then Strength brings up the question of when and how we need to tame ourselves. Of course, there is a certain amount of self-restraint required as a functioning member of society. We cannot murder, be naked in public, steal, etc. But there is a more nuanced self-mastery Strength speaks to which is at the core of its lesson.

When we connect the softness of the heart chakra with the fire of the sacral chakra, we arrive at Strength. Allowing for the healthy expression of sexuality, vitality and passion, this archetype affords the realization that we do not always need to bulldoze through a situation to be heard or get what we want. Aligning with this benevolent force facilitates the gentle expression of the will in a way that is both effective and merciful.

Sacred sexuality is a cornerstone of Strength. My dude Oscar Wilde said, "Everything in the world is about sex except sex. Sex is about power." Strength is the opposite of that. Ideally, sex is not a means to an end. It is aligning with our sexuality as a means of embodiment, pleasure and intimacy.

We cannot and should not rid ourselves of our wildness; to do so would flatline life itself. But this archetype offers us an opportunity to have dominion over it. We are no longer at its mercy and are only enriched because of it. In Strength, we reach a point where what we want to do and what we should do are the same, where the higher and lower self are not warring with conflicting desires, where we may tame destructive impulses and transmute them into creative ones.

How many times have we verbally slashed someone to pieces and justified it because what we said was true? How many times have we lashed out in anger and excused it because the recipient deserved it? How many times have we wielded our sexuality as a weapon and felt okay about it because we felt an emotional remove from the situation? Strength is the antidote to these behaviors. It allows for kindness in our honesty. Level-headedness in our anger. Openheartedness in our sexuality. It files off the jagged edges of the instincts that would otherwise tear us apart.

There are different views in the tarot community of the positioning of Strength and Justice. In some decks, Justice will appear as card eight with Strength showing up a bit later as card eleven. However, it makes sense to me that Strength shows up as the natural evolution from The Chariot and Justice as the middle point of the Major Arcana.

Anecdote

A few mornings ago I woke up with my heart racing at the length of my to-do list. We had an event at the store that evening, and there were a zillion tasks to complete in preparation for it, in addition to needing to drive my dog to the vet, answer some urgent e-mails, take a shower and finish a writing assignment. I was running the errands with a girlfriend who suggested stopping for coffee before we set out to conquer the day's tasks. We were already running late, and I had zero desire to kill any more time, but we all know that it is simply unwise to deprive caffeine addicts of their fix, especially if they're doing you a favor.

The coffee shop by our apartment is delicious and notoriously slow, but that morning it was next-level snail pace. The shop was virtually empty and we waited almost twenty minutes for our drinks. I was murderous. I was convinced the barista had some personal vendetta against me, considered complaining, asking for a manager, yelling at anyone who would listen, or making some passive-aggressive comment under my breath about how awful the service is at this place. But I also work at a shop and I (a) hate people who do shit like that and (b) don't really want to start beef with another local business. The consequences just weren't worth the savage satisfaction I would have gotten by being a nightmare in that moment. I took a breath, smiled and thanked the girl when our drinks came up and sprinted gold-medal-Olympics-style back to the car. We got everything done, and I can still show my face at my favorite coffee shop, shame-free.

In a Reading

Showing restraint. Having the maturity level necessary to handle a situation. Do not act rashly or out of anger. Reconciling the desires of the lower self—exhibiting self-control but also being satisfied. Sexual awakening and the healing of the sacral chakra. Issues with sexuality. Solving a problem by being patient. Understanding that some things just take time to do right. Being subtle in your power—using persuasion, influence and working with others rather than using force.

9—THE HERMIT

The cave you fear to enter holds the treasure you seek.
—Joseph Campbell

wisdom / self-study / solitude / internal / introspection / hibernation / aloneness / contemplation / illumination / retreat / gestation / misanthropic / meditation / searching / passage / seeker / true north / austere

Card Meaning

The Hermit is one of the scariest cards of the tarot for me. Some people dread Death, or The Tower, or one of the shitty Swords cards, but there is something about the solitude, introspection and stillness The Hermit asks of us that never fails to freak me the fuck out. This is not necessarily a universal sentiment. Our reaction to The Hermit's energy is commensurate to our relationship with solitude.

Even when I am alone, I still gravitate to some form of connection. I have an audio book playing, or the TV on, or my phone glued to my hand like a bionic limb. I don't sit well in quiet. The Hermit exhibits a discipline that many of us avoid or deem unnecessary or say we'll get to later. However, this is a Major Arcana card, an unavoidable lesson that we cannot move forward without. If we do not willingly enter this quiet space, we will still find ourselves in it one way or another.

While resistance is a natural response to The Hermit, he also speaks to our innate desire to know ourselves well and deeply. One of the holiest energies of the tarot, he has turned away from society and the material world in search of a more meaningful kinship with the divine. At this point, other people cannot help us. We've gathered advice, acquired teachers and formed an identity we can show to the world. In The Hermit we examine the authenticity of that identity and shed the false self.

What a revelation it would be to enter into the cave of self-study and discover that you actually like what you find. Self-love and self-acceptance is not possible without this process. So many of us believe that we are bad, or wrong, or fundamentally broken in some way. No one can be talked out of this by another. The only tonic is seeing ourselves for ourselves. There is so much that another person cannot give us, even if they try.

There is an emptiness we navigate, an imbalance that we cannot reconcile if we refuse the self-commitment of The Hermit. What is more, he also holds the key to a greater spiritual connection, where we cultivate a personal relationship with the divine that is all our own.

For those who are prone to isolation, The Hermit can be a sign that it is time to come out of your shell, especially if surrounded by cards of community or partnership.

In addition to solitary self-discovery, The Hermit can signify an experience that teaches us about ourselves or represent a spiritual mentor or guide. Unlike The Hierophant, The Hermit will not put himself in a public or visible position, but may be sought out or otherwise present himself to you.

The Hermit is almost always seen holding a lantern or light of some sort. In the aloneness, he discovered his divinity, his wholeness and his authentic self. It cannot be taken by someone else, because it was not given by someone else. When we access this, we are never lost again.

Anecdote

This last year I moved to North Carolina with a boyfriend. We bought a house, filled it with things and broke up shortly thereafter. After a few months of couch surfing I moved into an apartment, marking the first time I ever lived alone.

It was hell. I was so used to having someone there, it felt like there was a perpetual emptiness that I could not negotiate. I already had a couple good friends whom I spent a lot of time with, but eventually they left, and whenever I was alone, the scary void of aloneness crept in again. The impulse to reach for contact was so unconscious I was often surprised by it. Why was I on my phone, re-checking the same thing I'd just looked at a couple minutes before? Why is the TV on? Why did I just agree to hang out with someone when I'm exhausted and just want to sleep?

The shift was subtle and happened over such an extended period of time that I have a hard time pinpointing its genesis, but I started to love coming home to my own space and spending a night in. I wouldn't feel anxiety staying at home on the weekends. I cherished the rituals I created: lighting my candles and burning sage before settling onto the couch, taking long baths on Sunday night, building altars, making a pot of tea and mixing an oil blend before sitting down at my desk to work. I started to feel protective of my space and charged by the time I spent alone in it. Seeing who I was, by myself, night after night, I learned that I enjoyed that company.

In a Reading

Finding light within yourself. Spend more time alone. Finding comfort in solitude. May be an indication to remove yourself from your usual environment and go somewhere alone—a retreat, or a quiet vacation. Withdrawing from the external world. Not the time to enter into new relationships. Reaching for the divine. A teacher you may need to seek out or be invited into.

10—THE WHEEL OF FORTUNE

What if a demon were to creep after you one night, in your loneliest loneliness, and say,
"This life which you live must be lived by you once again and innumerable times more;
and every pain and joy and thought and sigh must come again to you, all in the same sequence.
The eternal hourglass will again and again be turned and you with it, dust of the dust!"
Would you throw yourself down and gnash your teeth and curse that demon?
Or would you answer, "Never have I heard anything more divine"?
—Nietzsche

repetition / inception / opportunity / destiny / rebirth / impermanence / cycle /
reincarnation / patterns / impartial / inevitable / interconnected / return / growth /
continuous / patterns / karma / time / luck

Card Meaning

There are a lot of cards in the tarot that represent the capacity for change, but none so fundamental as The Wheel of Fortune. When we invoke this energy in our lives, we become fully awake to patterns we repeat and are given an opportunity to break them. Even if we are

to some extent aware of the patterns, this archetype brings it to the surface in a way that is perhaps exaggerated or painfully acute. A little game-showy, a little creepy, it delivers our life back to us at a cinematic fever pitch that makes us cringe and say, "Wow, am I really still doing this shit?"

It can be traumatic to feel like we are back in the same place, but that is never the truth. If time is a spiral, we will find ourselves again and again at parallel points inside it; but each time we do we are closer to the center. When you arrive at one of these lateral coordinates, you can see the ways you have grown or refused growth. How are you different, and what are you capable of now that you weren't the last time? Can you, will you do better by yourself and others than before?

The Wheel of Fortune is one of the few cards that represents an energy and not a person, though a person may invite this energy into your life. Imbued with revolutionary potential, the choice presented to us in The Wheel of Fortune is rarely an easy one. Old habits die hard, and it is difficult to break one even if we know it will serve us. It should be both daunting and reassuring to know that, as far as the tarot is concerned, there are no missed opportunities. We can willfully ignore the cycle brought to our attention through this card and choose to repeat it—The Wheel will land on it again. But when it does it will be more glaring, with more accumulated consequences and higher stakes.

This sounds pretty doomsday-esque, but in truth we do this all the time. Chronic lateness, bad sleeping habits, unhealthy eating, partying too much. When we fail to rectify these patterns The Wheel of Fortune may appear in the form of missing an important meeting, or outgrowing a favorite pair of jeans. More seriously, it may show up as illness, self-sabotage or destroying something we hold dear.

In addition to our personal shitty behaviors, The Wheel of Fortune can also speak to karma, past lives, shadow inheritances and ancestral ties. It is not unusual for this card to show up in a reading as a chance to break a pattern that has followed their bloodline through generations.

Both Buddhism and Hinduism acknowledge the concept of reincarnation, and we could look at each spin of the wheel as a new lifetime. The ultimate goal is to not have to incarnate again, which means getting off the wheel in every way. Let's start small though, shall we? Every time we truly break a cycle, we dismantle that particular wheel. It will no longer leave us dizzy and nauseated because we are no longer reeling inside of it.

An alternate interpretation could be this card appearing during a time of uncertainty, where we took a gamble and are waiting on the result. If so, there is nothing to do but let the wheel stop spinning and see where it lands. Table your efforts and let the universe do its thing.

The Hermit unearthed the patterns presented to us in The Wheel of Fortune. We know ourselves, what lurks in our depths and what we are better off letting go of. While it can be humiliating and demoralizing to stay woke to our ugliest behaviors, The Wheel of Fortune is always a prayer answered. It facilitates an awareness called in by the higher self, the part of us that cares more about our betterment than temporary discomfort or embarrassment, and we are better for it.

Anecdote

I've cheated in almost every romantic relationship I've entered into. Yikes. That's not a cute sentence to write. I have a deep-seated destructive impulse that manifests as boredom, apathy, feeling trapped and basically wanting to burn down everything good in my life.

My last serious relationship was with a wonderful man whom I was absolutely in love with. About a year and a half into our relationship (typically the time I start to search for some gasoline and a match), I found myself alone in a room with a person who I was very much attracted to and would have loved to sleep with, and if there was ever an opportunity to do it, this was it. In the midst of the shadow demon-zilla in my mind that was screaming "do it" over and over again, there was another competing thought alongside it. If I cheat right now—on this man, with this person, in the relationship that I'm currently in—I will cheat in every relationship I have for the rest of my life. In past situations, I justified it for various reasons: I was unhappy, they were unhappy, the relationship wasn't working anyway. But there was no excuse here. I loved my boyfriend, everything was amazing between us, and I'd never been so happy or felt so seen by another person. I immediately left the room and took a long walk, waiting for demon-zilla to calm down. I felt the cycle break then and there, and honestly walking away from that immediate gratification was difficult. But it also allowed me to experience a love and connection with my partner stronger and more profound than anything that came before it because I had always gotten stuck in that wheel. Saying no in that moment, when so much of me wanted to say yes, showed me how to find a source of energy that wasn't the flames of something I love burning to the ground.

In a Reading

Karmic cycles. Reincarnation. Opportunity for major change. Invitation to break a pattern. Heightened awareness of your behaviors. Being tested. Waking up for a moment to the inner workings of the universe. The energy of luck. Taking a chance. Experiencing movement, though you may not be the one controlling the movement, you are in control of how you handle it.

11—JUSTICE

Measure twice, cut once.
—Proverb

integrity / consequence / balance / equality / perfection / centered / fairness / law / self-examination / leveling / stern / precise / unwavering / scales / conscience / values / unbiased / deliberation

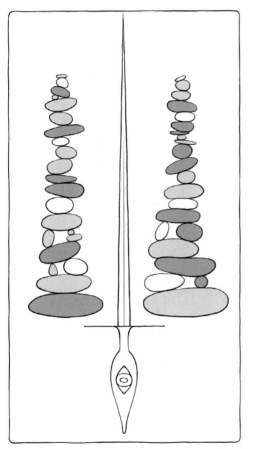

Card Meaning

With Justice, we arrive at the exact halfway point of the Major Arcana. We've been through some shit. In the words of Kylie Jenner we've, like, realized a lot of things, and at this middle place we stop and take stock.

Rarely does the Major Arcana borrow the suits of the Minor, but Justice is almost never seen without her sword. Representing cognition, analytical thought and all workings of the mind, Justice reflects a full-formed conception of self. The sword is ours to wield, we have done the work required to be entrusted with it. We have access to the full force of our mental body.

The representation of the mind as a sword offers a potent clue about its limitations. A sword is a weapon. In Justice, we have reached the highest possible potential of how we may wield it, but it is still only a sword. It does not transmute its nature as a cutting device.

So what does it look like when we can have faith in the efficacy of our minds and the soundness of our judgment? We arrive at Justice. We are able to cut things out of our life responsibly, make decisions ethically and rely on our personal system of checks and balances. We gathered our stamina in The Chariot, refined it in Strength, let it gestate in The Hermit

Hermit and had it tested through The Wheel of Fortune. At Justice we are standing in a place of balance and certainty of self. We earned that. In this moment, the ego exists in a state of perfect balance.

Justice is the embodiment of integrity and perfection. But she is also harsh, unyielding and critical. While she is an essential archetype and an indispensible tool, she is forever intertwined with the sharpness of the Swords. One of the most masculine females represented in the Major Arcana, she is not devoid of sentiment. Rather, she has integrated all of it—her passions, ethics, logic, experience—into a system by which she gauges a situation. Rarely does Justice reflect external institutions, though it can. It is a personal code that allows us to assess what we can and cannot live with.

There are times when societal justice does not align with personal justice. Abolitionists, civil rights workers and social justice activists are guided by this archetype. Here we can see the importance of cultivating this within ourselves, because society will, time and time again, collectively fail to achieve true justice. Inversely, we can also rely on her to take accountability when we've been wrong.

The harmonious meeting place of emotional intelligence and critical thought, Justice could be a second, more evolved incarnation of The Lovers. The feminine and masculine unify again with a purpose that serves more than themselves.

We utilize Justice to get back to balance. When we need to rid ourselves of something holding us back. We feel her in our innate yearning for equilibrium. We call upon her to help us fight for something we believe in. We return to her when we have betrayed ourselves, rely on her when we have strayed from our center and keep her counsel when faced with impossible choices.

And yet, reliance on intelligence alone will get us only so far. You see this in the constraints of Justice's capabilities and again when we pass through the journey of the Swords. From here, we move onto matters more broad and spiritual. The mind has taken us as far as it can. We must hone our other faculties—faith, fluidity, emotionality, intuition—to prepare for the mysterious and deeper second half of the tarot's Major Arcana.

Anecdote

When I decided to open Everyday Magic, I poured all of my heart and soul and energy and blood and sweat and tears and time into it. I'd been reading tarot for a couple of years and wanted to create a physical space to share the accouterments of magic that changed my life and the lives of my clients. I also grew up in a chaotic home, so the cultivation of a safe, sacred space has always been important to me, and I wanted to help others do the same. I was what some people would call "crazy" in how thoroughly I researched the integrity of our products. I sent vendors long lists of questions about how their materials were sourced, where they came from, how they were put together and the intention behind their wares. We turned away objects that were beautiful but made with unethically sourced leather, or adorned with exploitatively mined crystals. It was an exhausting and frustrating process, but it resulted in a space full of items we love, made by beautiful people with strong integrity and ethics. There is not an item that we sell at Everyday Magic that I cannot wholeheartedly get behind.

Shortly before we opened, we came under fire by a group of activists for cultural appropriation and contributing to the gentrification of the city I live in. Horrible things were said about me, my shop and my vendors—many of whom come from the cultural backgrounds these people claimed to protect. I specifically remember a comment along the lines of, "Who do they think they are to sell Zapotec textiles?" and thinking about the Zapotec women I bought them from, whose wares I paid fair wages for and who I spoke to for an hour about the process of making the weavings and what native plants, roots and produce they use to render each dye color. It ended with her putting me on my knees and blessing me, the textiles and the shop before we hugged and parted ways. I was devastated, upset and angry, but never once had to question if the accusations made held any weight. My integrity was my guide every step of the way in Everyday Magic's creation, and while we held space for the community to voice their concerns, I knew there was no apology owed. It was an overall horrible experience, but it was also eye-opening to find how much I trusted my ethics, my process and the decisions I made when they came under fire.

In a Reading
You can trust yourself. Using your mental faculties responsibly and constructively. Strong intellect. Fairness. Exercising your own moral code. Self-examination and analysis using rational thought. Not a time to give in to impulse—do what you know to be right. Interaction with legal systems. Bringing things into balance. Settling debts. Letting go of things if they do not align with your ethics. Carefully considering all sides of a situation before making a decision. The natural equilibrium of all things. Being accountable and taking responsibility if you fucked up.

12—THE HANGED MAN

The dead can hide beneath the ground and the birds can always fly
But the rest of us do what we must
in constant compromise.
Bright Eyes, *Middleman*

non-action / suspension / fear / wisdom / release/ non-attachment / surrender / initiation / shift / transformation / stuck / inversion / illumination / incubation / serene / acceptance / suffering / sacrifice / renunciation

Card Meaning
One of the more iconic cards of the tarot, The Hanged Man is always depicted as being suspended upside down. This inverted viewpoint is central to his wisdom, but the experience

of The Hanged Man varies depending on our perspective.

It is impossible to understand The Hanged Man without knowing it is the card that precludes Death. It therefore raises the question: How do we come to terms with death? How do we prepare for it? Reconcile its inevitability? The Hanged Man is the act of giving something permission to die, and this can be a time of profound acceptance and detachment. However, it can just as easily be mired with suffering, resistance and fear. Often, it is both.

Regardless of how we choose to meet The Hanged Man, he comes into our life and demands transformation, and it is specifically because of his closeness to Death that this transformation is possible. In Justice, we reached the apex of our analytical mind's potential; in The Hanged Man we transmute it altogether for the sake of going further. Because there is a feeling we cannot shake that there is something "more." Ideally, we willingly enter this sometimes uncomfortable initiation to discover what we are capable of becoming.

A snake does not mourn the loss of its old skin, nor does the caterpillar lament its chrysalis. There is wisdom found in the animal kingdom in their relationship to transformation. Resistance of The Hanged Man and the denial of Death are connected to the ego, which animals do not possess. It is only when we hold on for too long that this natural process becomes a place of suffering. It is interesting that to achieve a heightened state of consciousness we must set the ego aside in favor of something more primal than we'd care to admit and more divine than we can fathom. To grow, you must outgrow.

While The Hanged Man is a male archetype, in many ways he is the ultimate testament to the potency of feminine power. In this place of non-action, receptivity and surrender we change beyond what we ever imagined possible, a change that could never happen by manipulating or forcing an outcome. It is one of the most perfect examples in the tarot of something femininity does perfectly and that masculinity cannot scratch the surface of.

Every time I see The Hanged Man card my impulse is to turn him around, not because I don't know he's chilling exactly how he's supposed to, but because my brain wants things right side up. Society's response to this archetype is similar, and The Hanged Man can be met with criticism or bewilderment for his unusual views.

The health benefits of inversion are many—hanging upside down can relieve back pain, improve brain function and posture, increase circulation, strengthen your legs and core and clear your complexion. However, our bodies are meant to be feet-first on the ground, and if we stay there for too long we risk serious medical problems. The Hanged Man is not meant to be inhabited indefinitely. Detachment is necessary at times, but getting stuck in this energy can lead to depression, indifference and alienation.

Like a snake shedding its skin, The Hanged Man sheds only what is ready to leave us. When we let go of something, it should never feel like we are hacking off one of our own limbs. The tarot will not ask us to do something we are incapable of. In The Hanged Man, whatever we are leaving behind is also leaving us. It is the morning we wake up after a debilitating breakup and our ex isn't the first thing we think about when we open our eyes. It is an obsession that loosens its grasp, a spell that breaks. Ultimately, The Hanged Man brings freedom through expansion.

Anecdote

My relationship with my ex was dying long before either of us was ready to admit. It was no one's fault, or it was both our faults, or maybe it was the world's fault; there are so many things I can point to as possible reasons, but the facts were the same. We were roommates, best friends, dog co-parents and family, but the thing that makes a romantic relationship tick, that elusive but essential lifeblood, was gone. It left somewhere along the way, or we failed to properly nurture it. When we finally acknowledged this, we spent months trying to heal the damage and get back to a better place. When we couldn't do that, we went on a break—an ill-conceived, desperate attempt to hold on to each other that ended up hurting both of us even more.

The break was intended as a space for us to change in the ways that were required for our relationship to work again. It was a doomed mission. We spent most of it hating each other. He moved out and then I moved out and back in and then out again. I kept postponing the end-date we'd set to get back together because the idea of it sent me into a panic, but I also wouldn't look for a new place to live because it meant we were really over. This resulted in months of couch surfing, heartache, listlessness, fear and depression. I shut down my heart because it was too painful to feel it. I was a cold, removed, semi-robotic version of myself.

I don't regret this insane period of my life, but we sometimes wonder about the pain we could have saved ourselves by skipping the break and just letting it end.

In a Reading

Getting ready to release something. Letting go. Becoming aware that something in your life is dying. Coming to terms with death. Surrendering completely to an experience, even if it hurts. Suspending action and decisions. Resisting change. Suffering due to non-acceptance. Slowing down. A paradigm shift, or change in how we perceive reality. Depression. A sign to stop pushing against the current. Evolution or transformation, but the kind that happens by allowing it, not that you have to catalyze or control. Initiation—letting something end for the sake of eventual new beginnings.

13—DEATH

Grieve. So that you can be free to feel something else.
—Nayyirah Waheed, *Nejma*

transition / loss / natural / leveling / transformation / freedom / bare / impartial / return / refinement / letting go / metamorphosis / closure / release / bridge / inevitable

Card Meaning

With Death, we arrive at one of the most dreaded cards in the tarot. Because it is a card that has so much fear and negativity associated with it, readers are quick to dismiss the grittiness of Death and explain it as rebirth or transformation. The instinct is a kind one, but to do so does not fully honor the gravity of this card and cheapens the experience for people going through it. Yes, Death facilitates transformation. Yes, there is a natural rebirth that this cycle enables. But for either of those to take place, the dying needs to happen. It's a loss, and a significant one, and it probably fucking sucks. Even if it is graceful, dignified and right, there is inevitable pain that accompanies it.

Rarely does Death symbolize the physical death of a person, and I strongly advise exercising caution about interpreting this card literally. Usually, it shows up to signify the death of a relationship, job, behavior or part of ourselves. The spiritual concept of dying before you die is explored across religions and faiths, typically encouraging people to not shy away from the opportunity Death provides us to live a fuller, more authentic life.

The comfort of Death is that whatever is passing is no longer meant to live. It could be said that in Justice we have discovered what needs to die, in The Hanged Man we let go of it and in Death it leaves us. In addition to grief, there is often a sense of relief and rightness that accompanies this experience. When we defy death, when we hold on to something that no longer wants to be possessed, we still do not get to keep it. The thing in question will calcify, embodying The Devil's toxicity and destructive qualities before it is eventually shaken loose through The Tower. Knowing that something is meant to end does not necessarily make the ending easier, but it does provide context in a space where we could otherwise be swallowed whole by our grief.

It is human nature to avoid pain, but after Justice we passed the point of being beholden to just our human nature. This is a point that many people do not pass. They reach Justice and live in it, meet their mortality at The Hanged Man and experience Death once, at the end of their life. To achieve Justice is no small feat, for it allows a life of integrity, values

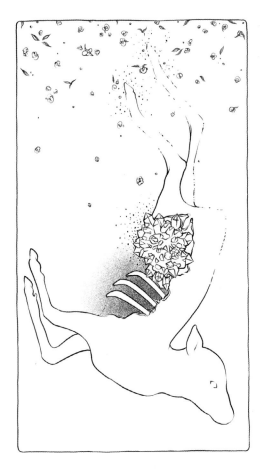

and balance, and it is no one's place to pass judgment on people who take this path. However, Death is far from the last card. Allowing this energy into our life makes room for the glorious cards yet to come. In my experience, they are not to be missed, and it is worth feeling all the pain that Death brings with it in order to continue on.

Anecdote

It will come as no surprise that the break with my ex did not end in us getting back together. I came to the house to see Zadie one evening, and we were sitting on the back porch when I told him that it wasn't going to work. I had no intention of saying it, no plan of coming over and putting us out of the misery of this break, but before I could formulate the thoughts, I was honest with him and myself for the first time.

I loved him. I was so afraid that I would never find love like that again. Never feel as at home and at ease with someone as I did with him. I told him that I loved his family and the family we created together over the last three and a half years. I told him I knew we could survive this break and get back together, and it might be fine for a while. But if I didn't leave now, I knew in the deepest part of myself that I would leave eventually, it was only a matter of when. It was information that came from a clear, true, ruthless voice inside me that would not be quieted or quelled.

After the animosity of the last few months, I expected a fight. He was quiet for a long time. And then he looked me in the eye and thanked me for finally setting us both free.

Everything I wouldn't let myself experience, the distant and unfeeling place I preserved myself in during our time apart, immediately melted, and I felt my heart break. It literally, viscerally felt like I took a sledgehammer and smashed the shit out of my heart. We spent the next three days in the house crying, holding each other, talking, processing and grieving. I could finally feel my love for him without resentment or hostility because I no longer needed him to be someone he wasn't. The grace, tenderness and consideration for each other in those few days spent together in mourning will forever be one of the most difficult and beautiful experiences of my life. While the pain was so extreme at times I was sure I would be crushed under its weight, there was no thought of reversing our decision, no wondering if we made a mistake. He is still one of my favorite people, closest friends and the best dog dad a girl could hope for.

In a Reading

I would be remiss to not discuss here how sensitive, painful and just overall soul-crushingly shitty the Death card can be for people. When this card shows up in a reading, I encourage the person I'm reading for to fortify themselves with support. This is going to suck. It's going to feel surreal. Reach out, take care of yourself, get support, seek solace in ritual, give yourself space to grieve, don't try to pretend like everything is okay. It's not. But it eventually will be. Something is dying, and yes, it's really over, even though that feels impossible.

14—TEMPERANCE

Wear your halo like a hat, that's like the latest fashion
I got angels all around me they keep me surrounded.
—Chance the Rapper, *Angels*

alchemy / moderation / balance / magic / divine protection / duality / gnosis / blending / sobriety / the middle way / devotion / guidance / grace / guardians / angels / healing / calm

Card Meaning

Temperance is a difficult energy to pinpoint because it manifests as the moments we have come into contact with grace and where spirit has intervened on our behalf. Therefore, we grow to understand Temperance in the things that didn't happen more than events that have come to pass. The person who was late to work at the World Trade Center on the morning of September 11th, who stayed home sick from school the day of the shooting. Every path we didn't take, every near miss, every calamity we never knew we avoided can be attributed to the angelic protection of Temperance.

In Temperance, we are standing in the presence of our guides, angels and ascended masters. We faced Death and are standing in its afterglow—where fire and water blend— where the pain has burned off, and we are left only with the healing and lightness of what we've made room for.

Traditionally representing virtues like moderation and sobriety, Temperance brings us back to balance in a way that is patently different than Justice. Where Justice wields her sword to pair down, Temperance calls for adding ingredients to achieve harmony. Sobriety is, by definition, an abstinence from a material ingredient. However, the use of substances could be considered a thing that subtracts, as it limits an individual's capacity and prevents true

presence and connection. In Temperance, matter is not commensurate to value. We can add ingredients that detract from a larger whole, just as we can subtract destructive and divisive forces to make something more complete. When I fell in love for the first time, it was a softening of every hard thing in me, but nothing was lost. What left me was sharpness, masks, defenses that I thought protected me but only kept me small and separate. What it made way for was a fullness, presence and an unprecedented sense of peace. This was a graceful dance, an effortless negotiation, the most potent yet gentle physical sensation of magic and alchemy I've ever experienced. In either case, Temperance does not use a sword to make these adjustments. Perhaps where Justice cuts, Temperance melts.

Justice is a mastery of our decision-making processes, whereas Temperance speaks to a utilization of the Higher Self, which surpasses cognition. A calming and healing presence, we can call upon her to aid in forgiveness, quell hysteria, diffuse volatility and enable creative problem solving.

We develop a relationship with Temperance when we begin to believe that the game of life is rigged in our favor. Her grace allows us to see the inherent benevolence of the universe. It is a Source that we can cultivate an immediate relationship with. She both reminds us that we are safe and ensures that safety on our behalf. There is an exalted, almost ecstatic energy Temperance brings when we allow her to work with us.

Temperance can come into our life as a divine intervention, or signify a visitation from a departed loved one or spirit guide that wishes to make their presence known. A friend's mother once found an old raincoat from her father's company in a store. Before discovering it, his favorite Frank Sinatra song came on and she could smell him in the air.

Positioned as the last card of the Major Arcana's second row, we are again brought to the precipice we first met at The Chariot. What kind of graduation does Temperance mean for us? If The Chariot is going off to college, then Temperance could be the completion of our PhD in life.

With all of this blissful angelic realness set aside, we cannot ignore that The Devil is the very next card. What meaning is added to Temperance when we consider its positioning? Perhaps its speaks to the precarious nature of her perfection. Or, it could be the solidifying agent for the spiritual foundation we need to face the deep-rooted and complex issues presented in The Devil.

Anecdote

I was a rebellious, addicted and suicidal teenager. Memories of my high school experience are mostly swallowed up by a black hole of depression and wishing that I didn't exist. With over a decade between me and my teenage years, I can safely say it was more than teen angst. I do not subscribe to the concepts of good and evil, but I was wrestling with something dark and karmic and destructive and powerful during that period of my life, and it was winning.

My mother was an addict and eventually took her own life as a result of her disease. While I was definitely a full-fledged addict by the time I was sixteen, there were some hard and fast rules I set for myself to justify my behaviors and, beyond that, differentiate myself from my mother. No hard drugs (loosely, loosely used definition) was rule number one. By the end of the first semester of my senior year in high school, I was ready to cross that line.

Every morning on the way to school my deadbeat friends and I would get supremely high, and it was a Friday shortly before Thanksgiving when I decided to buy some of the aforementioned hard drugs to take at a party that night. It would have been my first time.

When my dean and two police offers walked into my third period AP English class to escort me out, I was still too high to realize what was going on. In a dumb, dreamy state I watched them search my car and line up the contraband on the asphalt while a white moth—a symbol I've always associated with my mother—landed on my backpack.

I will never know what would have happened had we not been caught on our high school's security cameras that morning, still smoking a bowl as we pulled onto campus. There is a horrible possibility that lives alongside me getting arrested, going to rehab and getting sober that I did not have to live out, or die from.

In a Reading

Spiritual, divine or angelic intervention. Direct contact with your guides and masters. Being protected or overseen by a benevolent energy. Mediumship, a message from a departed loved one will make itself known through Temperance. Returning to your center. Choosing the middle way. Avoiding extremes. Combining different elements to achieve equilibrium. Finding the right mix. Adding elements rather than taking things away to solve a problem. A harmonious merging of seemingly opposing energies. A time of harmony and balance. A feeling of exhilaration, well-being, health and lightness after Death.

15—THE DEVIL

The soul is restless and furious; it wants to tear itself apart and cure itself from being human.
—Unknown

perversion / distortion / imbalance / addiction / succumbing / enslavement / blocked / vices / bondage / insidious / indulgent / seductive / karmic / deep-rooted / consumption / suffering / oppression / hedonism

Card Meaning

Another greatly feared and widely misunderstood archetype, The Devil brings us face to face with our deepest defects. The cycles we could not break in The Wheel of Fortune, cut away with Justice or surrender to Death reach their fever pitch in this difficult card.

We aren't still holding on to these blocks due to laziness or deficiency. This is some primo shit. Our bodies grew around these blocks. They reside in the very marrow of our bones, are embedded in our souls and our psyches. They are wounds we were born with, or that were inflicted early and often, before we could properly defend and protect ourselves, and have since festered and metastasized. Now they are so insidious that we often confuse them as facts of who we are. There is no quick fix, no neat extraction for The Devil. When it leaves us, it is under fire. The Devil unearths these wounds for us so that they may then be seared away by The Tower, and honestly it's probably going to be a hot mess.

The Devil is a relationship gone toxic, whether it is with a person, substance, behavior or object. It is the perverse relative of The Lovers and a false iteration of The Sun. Manifesting as addiction, abuse and excess of all sorts, we do not fully appreciate the power of The Devil until first coming to terms with his insidiousness. The Devil is not a monster that jumps in our path baring his teeth and snarling at us. If he did, then we'd be like, "Damn, I better get this under control." Rather, The Devil makes us think that he is our friend. That he alone protects us, understands us, comforts us and keeps us safe. People are very attached to their Devil. You will often hear alcoholics say, "Alcohol wasn't my problem: it was my solution." The moment we start to question this is the moment we begin to invoke our own freedom.

And yet, the seductive draw of The Devil is undeniable. Its message is that we are in bondage, and sometimes that's really fucking hot. With the constant demands, pressure and responsibilities that accompany being a grown-up person, there is an innate craving to just give in to what feels good—to give up control or to wield complete control. To do so can allow for intense creative expression and sexual energy. BDSM culture, for example, builds a container for the shadow aspect of our selves craving that power dynamic. But that is a conscious and consensual exploit. The Devil does not ask our permission. Often, we don't even know he is there, pulling our strings from the shadows.

When we get to the bottom of The Devil's manifestation in our life, we will often find a hurt inner child. A wounded fragment of ourselves that chipped off and got amber-trapped in time. It may still be active in our life because we have denied its existence, or met it with hostility when nurturing was called for.

The Devil's origin is a natural one, a need or desire that has grown out of control. A love of the sun can lead to cancer if used to excess. When we identify our false needs (for example, an alcoholic does not need alcohol, even though they may truly believe they do), we find our shadow selves. In Jungian psychology, the shadow is defined as any part of ourselves that dwells beyond our conscious minds. This can include our primal nature, taboo desires, creative aspirations, a feeling of lack. Anything that we deem unacceptable, that we cannot reconcile with our sense of self, gets stored in the shadow. In Jung's words, "The less it is embodied in the individual's conscious life, the blacker and denser it is." The Devil marks the inevitable point where the shadow refuses to remain suppressed, often to destructive results. There are healthy expressions of the shadow self if we are willing to accept it and get to know that part of ourselves.

The Devil begs a question, and it's a sexy one. Does he want us to pass the test he gives us? My feeling is that he does. He reveals us to ourselves in a way that no card preceding it could. He brings us to our knees, connects us to a sense of humility that we both violently reject and essentially require. He excavates his manifestations for us to clear should we wish to continue on.

Anecdote

The first time I smoked a cigarette, I was fifteen years old, in my boyfriend's garage in the middle of an especially brutal Chicago winter. He and his friends would migrate from the basement to the garage to smoke cigarettes in the bitter cold, and anyone who has endured a Midwest winter will tell you that you do not go outside in the minus 20–degree windchill for no reason. So I decided, what the hell, I might as well just smoke one of the things as an excuse to go outside with them.

Dear fifteen-year-old Bakara, you are an idiot. I honestly hate you for this shortsighted, reckless, irreversible decision you made to fit in with a guy who would fade into obscurity a few months later. Out of all the stupid, dangerous shit you did in your dumbass teenage years, this is the one I most wish I could have saved you from.

A very short while after my first cigarette, this dude was gone. But twelve years later, I'm still a smoker. A real smoker. Like if I leave the house and don't have them with me I'll go out and buy a pack kind of smoker. Like even if I'm around people who I know hate smoking and will think less of me for doing it I'll still smoke type of smoker.

Most of the time I think of cigarettes as a punctuation mark in my day. It is my reward for finishing a task, my respite when I need some time to myself, a peaceful break after a meal, a ritual before bed. Over the years I have probably contextualized my smoking in a thousand different ways. But in the occasional, lucid moments, I know it is none of those things. It is a toxin that I am viciously dependent on, something that hurts me every time I use it, a fuck you to myself, a way of saying no to life. It is a means of indulging the vague resentment I feel about the drudgery of being alive, a rebelling against myself to no end. And then I go unconscious again because the genesis of this behavior is so complicated that I am scared of what will be unearthed if I try to uproot it.

I've kicked a lot of addictions, broken some bad habits, put old patterns to bed. But my relationship with cigarettes continues to have an ironclad stronghold on my psyche.

In a Reading

The topic in question has become toxic. Addiction. Excess and overindulgence. Obsession. An abusive relationship. Materialism. Hedonism. Destructive behavior. False need. Saying no to life. Disconnected from spirituality and our divine source. Surrendering to pleasure, vices and indulgence. The shadow self at play. Powerlessness. Feeling trapped or denial of being trapped. Though denial is a common defense to further The Devil's workings, it does not appear in a reading unless we are ready to see it.

16—THE TOWER

Enlightenment is a destructive process. It has nothing to do with becoming better or being happier. Enlightenment is the crumbling away of untruth. It's seeing through the facade of pretence. It's the complete eradication of everything we imagined to be true.
—Adyashanti

destruction / burn / purification / release / upheaval / liberation / enlightenment / cataclysmic / transform / uproot / disintegration / apocalyptic / extreme / helplessness / chaos / turbulence / dismantling / calamity / violence

Card Meaning

Okay guys, shit is hitting the fan. There is no way around it. The Tower offers no quick fix, no neat solution, no way of pretending that everything is okay. Our life is ablaze, and the only option is to offer ourselves to the fire.

We are aware of how The Devil is holding us back. We maybe have stewed in it, faced extreme consequences because of it, felt how our well-being is compromised due to its presence or hit bottom as a result of its manifestations. The Tower is the prayer for freedom answered, whatever it takes. The willingness to do anything necessary is requisite, because The Devil's wounds are deep, and The Tower will rip us open to our core to extract them.

As I write this, forest fires are eviscerating the western part of my state. Whole mountains, old woods, people's homes, entire ecosystems and habitats are burning. It's been weeks of this. Wind has carried the smoke over two hundred miles east, and it looms over our city. The best efforts of thousands of people and the marvels of modern technology have not been able to extinguish it. We are all praying for rain.

This fire is awesome in its scope, non-negotiable, destructive beyond belief and a nightmare for the ones who are experiencing loss as a result. And yet, the fire is not cruel. The fire has no malice. In fact, the ecological benefits of forest fires are numerous. It burns away undergrowth, allowing sunlight to reach the forest floor, removes alien and parasitic species competing with native plants; replenishes and fertilizes soil. They are essential catalysts for supporting healthy ecosystems and biological diversity. The destruction ultimately facilitates the expansion of wildlife populations and provides a nutrient base for new growth.

This doesn't mean we cannot hate The Tower while it is happening. We wouldn't be human if we didn't struggle with this extreme energy. But when we step out of it, when we get some distance for it, we maybe find ourselves grateful. At the very least, we are not the same person we were when we entered it. The Tower is best appreciated in hindsight because in this urgent space we cannot reflect or search for greater meaning. It may be the greatest teacher of true and undivided presence because of its absolute consumption. If god dwells only in the present moment, it could be said that, for better or worse, we are never closer to the divine than we are when experiencing The Tower.

If Death is the peaceful passing of an old relative, then The Tower is the unexpected death of a young friend. For all of the purification properties of this archetype, we do not do it justice if we overlook the tragedy, calamity and shock this card can bring with it. Even the staunchest believers in "everything happens for a reason" will have their faith tested in The Tower. It can show up in ways that feel inexplicable, unfair and impossible. And yet, it's not the end, and there is greater light ahead as we move on to the final few cards of the Major Arcana.

Seneca the Younger said, "Fire proves gold, adversity proves men," and in The Tower, we walk through the fire. Whether we entered willingly or were forced in kicking and screaming, the effect is the same. It scorches off everything flammable, all that did not truly belong to us. Everything false is destroyed. We are left only with ourselves.

Anecdote

There are a few rules in rehab. Actually there's only two. While in rehab, don't sleep with any of your fellow rehab inmates and don't do drugs. Considering most people come to rehab with fried brains and ruined psyches, I appreciate them keeping it simple. However, I was incapable of following even these basic instructions. It took approximately a week for me to hook up with your friendly neighborhood heroin addict, and it took two and a half for me to go over to Jenna's house and drop acid with her.

If you've never done acid before, first of all, good for you, and second of all, the effects can last up to twelve hours, and I was in hell for every single one of them. I resolved to be substance free for the duration of my rehab program, to show everyone that I was so fine and totally not addicted to drugs and could stop whenever I wanted. And there I was, lying on the floor of her basement, tripping absolute balls and waiting for it to end.

When it finally did end, I drove home. It was a snowy December morning, and so bone-chillingly cold outside I could feel it creeping into the windows even with the heat on full blast. Who did I need to lie to? What did I tell my parents to explain me getting home at 7 a.m., an hour I was (and still am) rarely awake for? How did I hide this from my rehab?

I went through it in my head. Acid doesn't show up on a drug test. I crafted a passable lie to tell my parents. No one needed to know this happened. It could just be another fuckup, another lie, another thing that I had to lock up in the box of secrets I carried around with me. I was so tired, so broken, so short-circuited from the nightmare of the evening's events, I planned on going home and sleeping into the next morning.

Less than a block away from my house is a train track, and as I pulled up to it, the crossing guards came down. I cursed the gods and hoped it wasn't a freight. But nothing came. At all. For well over thirty minutes, the gates stayed down to protect us from a ghost train that never came.

I'd already been arrested, kicked out of school and forced into rehab. Before that I'd lost weight, friendships and the perfect GPA that mattered so much to me in school. My writing was at a standstill, and my college applications were in jeopardy because of the legal trouble I found myself in. The Tower went into effect before this exact moment, but in that car, that freezing morning, a block away from home—I finally felt it. I didn't want another secret to keep, another lie to tell. I didn't want it to be like this anymore. And all of a sudden, for the first time, it was apparent that it didn't have to be. Everything would have to change, but it could be different.

Everything did change that morning. It marked the beginning of a seven-year period of sobriety and an exorcism of the dark thing in me. It has not returned since.

In a Reading

Major disruption and upheaval. Shit's going down. Sudden change. Being brought to your knees. Humility/humiliation. Spiritual awakening. A massive energetic release—explosion or outburst. Annihilation of the ego. Destruction of the false self. The thing in question is not long for this world; it is meant to burn. Crisis. Tragedy. Freeing yourself from something at all costs. A burst of awareness. A realization that requires dismantling your current reality.

17—THE STAR

A philosopher once said, "Are we human because we gaze at the stars, or do we gaze at them because we are human?" Pointless, really. Do the stars gaze back? Now, THAT's a question.
—Neil Gaiman, *Stardust*

healing / hope / connection / altruism / wish / divine navigation / rebuild / wellspring / salvage / inspiration / recovery / new dawn / illuminating / cleansing / destiny / guided

Card Meaning

We just got the shit kicked out of us by The Tower. We are tired and broken and probably still covered in ash. When the last ember extinguishes itself, when the smoke clears, when the dust settles, we enter into The Star. She is shimmering, hydrating, healing. She gives us water, puts salve on our burns and offers us refuge. If it is always darkest before the dawn, then The Star is that dawn. Think about the hardest you've ever cried in your life, and then the moment you took a deep breath, wiped the snot off your face and decided you were done crying. You feel lighter. And clean. That is The Star.

This doesn't mean that everything is better, that all problems are solved and questions answered. But the problems and questions that seemed baffling up until this point don't feel so unfathomable anymore. We know how to proceed, we know what we need to do, and we feel connected to a newfound sense of purpose. We fought hard for this wisdom. We cleaned out the gutters of our ego so that water may flow freely through it. We found the "on" button to the divine navigation system we didn't know came with the basic model. And while we're

so fucking exhausted, we're also hopeful, even exhilarated, basking in The Star's peaceful glow.

After the rapid-fire action of the preceding cards, The Star asks us to chill for a sec and nourish ourselves. We know we're going to be okay, we know we're going to regroup and rebuild, but here we recover. If we didn't know how to take care of ourselves before, this is where we learn.

The Star is a gorgeous card, one that offers us respite and renewal while allowing us to reflect on our resilience. In The Tower, we might have been sure we wouldn't survive it, that it took everything and left us bare. But if The Tower is the difficult and excruciating labor, then The Star is the merciful birth. And here we are, fortified and clear, not broken and empty. We may feel a quiet sense of fearlessness as we are baptized in The Star's healing waters.

The Star gives us a glimpse into an unknown part of ourselves which we can have faith in and depend upon. We opted for Death, faced The Devil and released it in The Tower. This is not for nothing. The payoff we go on to find is our capacity to irrigate and nourish the world around us. We are strong in our purpose. We sense our creator's presence in all that we do. We sense our intended contribution to the world and feel drawn to manifest it. We have identified a North Star, and although its directions may frighten us, we know it will never, ever steer us wrong.

Anecdote

I was invited to sit in a Shamanic medicine ceremony after years of hoping for the opportunity to participate in one. Long story short, I came excited and left half-dead. It was, without question, the most terrifying, painful, guttingly soul-wrenching evening of my life. Every nightmare I ever had, every fear that dwelled in my unconscious, every unresolved thing in my heart was brutally excavated and then experienced. There were whole swaths of time where my grasp on reality was lost, and I was convinced I would never escape this fever dream. Never in my life have I been stripped so bare. I prayed for the medicine to kill me.

The medicine ran through me, the sun rose and sanity returned. I felt empty and light.

The horror of the night before was so intense I was convinced I would never live through it, and yet it was already leaving me. The horror was replaced with relief and then exhilaration. Though it was in a safe container, it was the first time I experienced surviving something I thought I wouldn't. Wrapped in a blanket at sunrise, warmed by a bonfire, I kept thinking, "If I can get through that, there is nothing left to be afraid of."

In a Reading

Regaining hope. Looking toward the future. Light at the end of the tunnel. Seeing your strength in hindsight. When you feel guided, something maybe should feel crazy or scary but it doesn't. Divine navigation system. Renewal of energy to continue on. Taking time to recover. Feeling like you are in the right place in the world. Connecting with true purpose. Generosity. Feeling what you have to offer others. A period of peace, calm, tranquility and serenity—especially pronounced due to how starkly it contrasts with the chaos that preceded it.

18—THE MOON

We need the tonic of wildness . . . At the same time that we are earnest to explore and learn all things, we require that all things be mysterious and unexplorable, that land and sea be indefinitely wild, unsurveyed and unfathomed by us because unfathomable. We can never have enough of nature.
—Henry David Thoreau, *Walden*

reflection / receptivity / wild feminine / subconscious / mother /
intuition / phases / mystery / night / wildness / lunacy / madness / shadow / illogical /
complex / darkness / nature / hidden / dreams / instinct

Card Meaning

I have heard that the last row of the Major Arcana speaks more to overall environments than individual energies. It is an interesting idea, and one that makes sense given the fact that the further we travel down The Fool's Journey, the more expansive and ethereal the archetypes become. If we accept this theory, it is worth assessing who lives in these final few cards. The Wheel of Fortune's taunting repetition could reign from The Devil. The Hanged man, with his uncomfortable transformation could call The Tower his home. The Lovers could reside in the optimism and warmth of The Star. But the essentially feminine cards—The High Priestess and The Empress—belong to The Moon. She is their mother, their wellspring and the highest and vastest manifestation of the wild feminine.

This card has been long associated with madness, fear, darkness and deception, but I don't buy it. What we find in The Moon is ourselves, The Tower's purifying flames made sure of that. The negative associations The Moon has come to embody speak to a deficient and malnourished relationship with wildness.

A common depiction of this card shows two animals—dogs or wolves—howling at the moon. Because animals are without ego or preconceptions, this is an act of pure instinct. What would it take for us to do the same, to set aside our egos completely and fully give in to our wildness? It's understandable that this could inspire fear in many, but there is a reason The Moon is one of the last cards. The cards before it ensured that we have refined our instincts, pared away false needs and integrated the lower self whose impulses would cause harm. To fear The Moon would be to succumb to illusion, to jump at our own shadow. If The Devil elucidates the darkness of the lower self, then The Moon reflects the glimmering mysteries still locked within the higher self.

The physicality of wildness has been a longtime source of shame. Women are conditioned to shave or wax their body hair, hide signs of aging and use makeup to mask imperfection. The taboo and shame around wild sex prevent many from being honest about their sexual preferences. Children are punished for acting wild. The Moon is a place of great depth and takes a long time for us to come to terms with, but it's always been a room in our house. Before we know the true function of The Moon, it is easy to use it as a storage space wherein we throw everything we don't want, everything we don't know how to deal with, everything we're embarrassed about or fear we cannot show the world. By the time we consciously enter The Moon, we find it full of these unpacked boxes of shame and secrets. Here we must heed my dude Nietzsche's warning to "be careful, lest in casting out your demon you exorcise the best thing in you."

The things we discover in The Moon are not extraneous—what lives in this place are crucial tools for healership. We may feel a kneejerk reaction to place distance between us and our Moon qualities, but to do so deprives us of resources that make it possible to help others. We must remember that everything after The Tower serves to connect us to greater purpose, of harnessing both our light and dark to do the most good we possibly can in the world. When we free ourselves from shame and claim our nature we give other people permission to do the same by the sheer fact of our wild existence. Not everyone may identify as intuitive, but everyone can sense inauthenticity. I believe that to be a healer you don't have to be living a perfect life, you don't need to have your shit together, you don't need to be in a flawless relationship or drink a green juice every morning, but you do need to be doing your work right alongside the people you are helping. In short, the most crucial requirement for being a healer is to be at peace with The Moon. When we unpack these boxes and share these secrets, we learn to love the powerful medicine she offers us. Like the moon itself, seeing the light in this part of ourselves is dependent upon external reflection.

While the idea of structure is a conventionally masculine notion, in The Moon we see its feminine expressions. The tides and behavior of animals are linked to its phases. There is a structure in the wild that exists beyond rationality. The perfection of the spider's web or bee's hive, the flight patterns of birds, the nesting behaviors of sea turtles—there is a knowledge ingrained in the very DNA of living things. What wisdom would we find if we moved beyond what we've been taught and leaned into the information encoded in our bones?

Anecdote

One summer night in Brooklyn, I found myself in Prospect Park with a group of friends. We were doing a ritual and finishing it by finding a tree to bury the materials we worked with. But wait, it gets weirder.

We found ourselves at the edge of a large clearing of grass, and though it was well after midnight, the sky was bright orange, with the full moon beaming silver behind misty clouds. At the same time, people kicked off their shoes and ran toward the middle of the field. Normally, this is where I go home. Being barefoot in a public New York area sounds like my personal hell. But I saw my friends running, dancing, howling, doing cartwheels, rolling around, and the primal energy of it was contagious. I started slow. I worried about looking stupid. When I accepted no one was looking, the release built, and I let my body move the way it wanted to, let noise escape my throat without censoring it. Sometimes I met another body and we moved together before fluidly parting. We stayed like that for a long time, ending in a pile on the grass together. Existing spontaneously, completely unregulated, if even for a short time, unlocked an ecstacy that I censor at every turn. It was trance-like. I felt high off that night for days. Even now, I return to that memory and hear it whisper back to me, calling me home again.

In a Reading

The wild feminine. Connecting to wilderness and nature. Complete release. Embracing the higher shadow self. Being ruled by impulse. Madness as medicine. Our subconscious and unconscious minds. The lizard brain. The ways in which we are like animals. Lack of ego regulation. Stop worrying about what you look like to other people. Lack of clarity, things that are unseen. The things that we bury. Needing to dig to find the truth. Dreams and dreamscapes.

19—THE SUN

I have sometimes thought that the reason the trees are so quiet in the summer is that they are in a sort of ecstasy; it is in winter, when the biologists tell us they sleep, that they are most awake, because the sun is gone and they are addicts without their drug, sleeping restlessly and often waking, walking the dark corridors of forests searching for the sun.

—Gene Wolf, *Peace*

pleasure / community / illumination / joy / innocence / energy / bursting / jovial / abrasive / freedom / aliveness / radiate / paternal / vitality / presence / youth / vibrant / relief / radiance / goodness / celebratory / confidence

Card Meaning

The Sun is a welcome sight in any reading, and some much needed ease after the tarot's most difficult stretch. His warmth offers us relief and clarity. The feeling of The Sun surpasses contentment and brings us to giddiness. We are reconnected with a sense of play. We are different for what we have been through, but The Sun's youthful energy enlivens us after a dense and demanding journey.

While The Sun is a light card, it is not a trivial one. The Fool is joyous and playful because it is his nature—he knows nothing else. But we arrive at The Sun after an extended period of darkness, with a renewed appreciation for life and a hard-earned understanding of this card's value. We are fully awake to the precious, healing nature of this oasis.

The Sun is benevolent but also impersonal. It indiscriminately nourishes everything and everyone it touches. However, it can also scorch, sicken and make arid if overused. Because it is unyielding in its energetic output, each person must negotiate his or her relationship to this archetype. Representing the highest potential of masculine expression, The Sun uplifts the ego, empowers the individual and fulfills the paternal needs of its recipient. Shadow, confusion and obscurity cannot exist in the blazing light of The Sun. And yet so many of the cards preceding it aided in the extraction, purification and integration of the shadow self.

Completing the last and most boundless power couple of the Major Arcana, the relationship between The Moon and The Sun is the oldest and most iconic love story of all time. The Sun drenches everything within its reach in light, which we sometimes need. However, the relief this light brings with it is contextualized by the shadows of The Moon. They work together in light and dark, lifting up the best of our feminine and masculine energies alike, and do not compete with each other or feel insecure about their roles. Their generosity and reciprocity with each other is so effortless, so natural, that it not only sustains them but also—quite literally—makes the world go round.

In addition to being inextricably connected to The Moon's complementary energy, The Sun also shares a relationship with The Devil—with the latter trapping a piece of the former's light and distorting its manifestations. Though they use it very differently, the energetic source is the same. Where The Devil is insatiable in his consumption, The Sun is incessant in his output. To live by The Sun is to live a natural life—he wakes up at sunrise (without an alarm because his circadian rhythm is so on point), makes a green smoothie and goes on a three mile run before work, whereas The Devil's up all night partying under artificial light and then sleeps half the day. But it could be said that the desire is the same—play, joy, pleasure. While we may find these things in The Devil temporarily, The Sun is the only true sustainable source of light, the embodiment of what The Devil looks for in places he will never find it. There is tragedy in this, but it is precisely because we passed through The Devil that we can be fully present for and appreciative of The Sun.

Anecdote

The few months before Everyday Magic opened consisted of twelve- to fifteen-hour work days, seven days a week. My partner in crime Madison and I sat at my dining room table every morning and often didn't get up until well after dark. Well, she got up, because she had to go home. I worked into the early hours of the morning, and when I finally made it to sleep I woke up repeatedly, mind buzzing with orders, paperwork and deliveries.

In the final couple days before the opening, Madison and I found ourselves tracking down missing packages at a FedEx warehouse that was impossibly huge and eerily empty. It looked like a place where people get murdered and their bodies are never found. We were delirious, overworked, underslept and poor. When we finally located our packages, hours later, we were driving back and pulled up at a red light alongside a taxi. It was an especially bright shade of yellow and sported bold black checkers. I turned to Madison and said, "Hey, look at that enthusiastic taxi," and for some reason it was the funniest thing either of us ever heard. We laughed for twenty minutes straight. Tears streaming down our face, muscles hurting, stomachache kind of laughter. Every time we thought we were done, we were swept up in another wave of hysteria. It was medicine. It sliced easily through the seriousness and intensity of our current situation and let us just be kids for a moment.

In a Reading

Joy. Being playful and silly as an adult. Relief after a lot of intensity. Appreciation of the moments of lightness. Carefree timelessness. Vacation. The truth coming out. Long awaited clarity. Moving or travelling to a warmer climate. Feeling energized/rejuvenated. Good vibes. Physical vitality. Doing fun shit. Experiencing expansion.

20—JUDGMENT

Forgiveness doesn't just sit there like a pretty boy in a bar. Forgiveness is the old fat guy you have to haul up the hill. You have to say I am forgiven again and again until it becomes the story you believe about yourself. Every last one of us has the capacity to do that, you included.
—Cheryl Strayed, *Tiny Beautiful Things: Advice on Love and Life from Dear Sugar*

integration / awakening / calling / rebirth / forgiveness / renewal / triumph / consciousness / purpose / ascension / healership / breakthrough / humbling / compassion / beacon / passage / levity / resurrection / reconciliation

Card Meaning

In The Star we got a glimpse of our purpose in the world; in Judgment, we live in that purpose. We are armed with a sense of self earned through experience and informed by our spiritual endeavors. We can track our evolution and are aware in Judgment that we are living in the payoff of the work we've done. We're confident but humble, driven but unrushed, grounded but also divinely guided. In Judgment we are reborn into the truest, best version of ourselves. We have our light and our dark, our masculinity and femininity, our spirituality and sexuality at our full disposal along with a vision of how to harness it all for our highest good.

An androgynous energy like The Lovers, Death and The Wheel of Fortune, Judgment is the ultimate healing of duality. It is true there is no other, within us or outside of us. There is no warring between the higher and lower self or tension between the ego and the heart. There is a place for all of it. The ego is satisfied, the needs of the lower self are met and the higher self is at work in the world. We've not only reconciled all that we are, but we find it glorious. We can see the light that shines through the cracks of our humanity and can do the same for others as a result. We are the person we worked to become. We are awake to our life's work and are using our leadership to heal, uplift and better the world around us.

Judgment represents our last task before we rest in The World, and it's a big one. It speaks to a forgiveness that is so radical in nature and vast in scope that it allows us to see ourselves in absolutely anyone. You can show mercy to people who Justice deems unworthy. You can disarm hatred. You can look at people who commit heinous acts and still see the humanity behind their crimes. This doesn't mean they're your bestie, or your boyfriend, but they could be a client. False grace will not work here. Real, genuine, search-the-depths-of-your-soul-to-see-if-you're-capable-of-this forgiveness is the best and only option. I've read for

clients who have done things that make my skin crawl, but it is not my place to judge them. The cards will take them to task if needed. If I shamed them or refused the reading because their behavior does not align with my morality, I miss a chance to help them. Rejection and punishment are not lasting catalysts for change. Judgment exists to bring other people into higher consciousness, a feat only unconditional love can accomplish.

People are naturally drawn to those who embody Judgment because, ironically, they don't feel judged in their presence. The word judgment can be an off-putting one and is rife with negative connotations, but human judgment has no role in this card. On the proverbial judgment day we rise, atone and ascend. Pseudo-creepy zombie-esque connotations aside, this card is defined by self-forgiveness and acceptance. We are putting the past and its hold on us to rest. We can use it as a tool to help others, can transmute it into wisdom and inform our decisions, but it does not own us, doesn't pull our strings from the shadows or dictate our impulses. This does not happen by shutting the door or trying to forget, but by meeting our stories and these old versions of ourselves with love and compassion.

This energy obliterates illusions of lack and scarcity and imparts the understanding that the more we give away, the more we gain. The power we claim is unique to us, and it is intuitive to be generous with others in this place. Buddha said it best, "Thousands of candles can be lighted from a single candle, and the life of the candle will not be shortened." We do not need to protect what is ours. Even if someone stole the safe, they do not have the code. Judgment is not susceptible to the pitfalls of power like we sometimes see in The Emperor or The Hierophant. We have found the outlet in the universe that fits our plug. We are incorruptibly fueled by our creator.

First and foremost, Judgment is a calling. What does it mean to be called, and how does it feel? What would motivate someone to resist a calling, or delay following it? A tarot reading digs through layers of fear and sediment into someone's core. When you are looking into their spiritual heart, you will find their personal Judgment. I've read for people who I don't like, whose personalities annoy me and whose politics I disagree with, but goddamn it is impossible not to fall in love with a person when you see this part of them. There is fear that following their calling will disrupt their life (which might be true), or that they aren't capable of it (not true) or are unwilling to accept it because they feel unworthy of their bigness (never true). It is the responsibility of those who have awoken to Judgment to reflect it back to others. You may not be a professional tarot reader, and that's chill. Maybe you work in tech or at a restaurant or at a bank or in marketing. But don't get it twisted. We are all healers, and Judgment injects healership into all that we do. Be willing to believe it. Be open to the possibility that you are bigger, more magical, more powerful than you dare imagine, that you are here to do something that is necessary and consequential and that only you can do. To say no to it not only robs your life of depth and meaning, it deprives others of the opportunity to benefit from you being your glorious, dazzling, badass best self.

Anecdote

For months, I waited and waited to give a reading that would be completely wrong. Every time I sat down with a client I thought, "This has gotta be the one." I was convinced, despite the strong connection I felt with the cards, that I was a fraud—I was just meeting people and using my powers of manipulation and persuasion to make them believe I was telling them something useful. I was holding on to the last shreds of my skepticism, still wrestling with the idea that a deck of cards could accurately speak someone's truth back to them. As soon as I sat down with a client, the fear left me, but the ten minutes before each reading was all-consuming anxiety. The first time I didn't experience this, my client was the most unlike-me person I'd seen at that point. He was a Puerto Rican man in his mid-sixties, a former New York City police officer, a grandfather and a widower.

There was absolutely no way I could even begin to fathom this man's experience. I couldn't fake it even if I tried, so I didn't try. I sat down with him and the cards left us both in tears. I got out of the way and let the tarot do its thing and it offered wisdom to both of us. I no longer doubt myself as a reader. I can be wrong—in fact, I'm wrong all the time. But the cards just aren't. And maybe that is completely fucking crazy, but if seeing is believing, I've seen hundreds of clients over the course of years, seen the tarot be so on point time after time, I do not have a single iota of doubt left in me that shit actually works. I can read for people who are nothing like me because they are not coming to me for my advice or experience; they are coming because they trust my ability to channel divine information for them honestly, clearly and with integrity. And I trust myself to do that, too.

In a Reading

Being called. Living in your healership. Being of service to others. Humanitarianism and philanthropy. Bringing others into the light. Fulfilling your purpose and life's work. Unburdening yourself from the past. Exercising mercy and forgiveness. Living a big, glorious, meaningful, full life. Personal reckoning. Facing yourself and liking what you see. Knowing your own goodness. Using your power for the highest possible service.

21—THE WORLD

Everything will be okay in the end. If it's not okay, it's not the end.

—John Lennon

completion / home / bliss / closure / supreme / future / belonging / harmony / arrival / womb / cosmic / abundance / success / contentment / source / encompassing / fullness / rest / ending / restoration

Card Meaning

We made it, fam. Pack your swimsuit and get ready for some R&R, fruity drinks served in coconuts, trashy vacation reads and long naps on the beach (that's how the saying goes, right?). In The World, we fall to our knees and kiss the hallowed ground we stand upon.

We have completed something major and The World invites us to bask in our contentment at a job well done. There is nothing to do, no outstanding tasks or loose ends or ongoing projects. We're really, really done. If Temperance and The Star are winter and spring breaks amid the grueling semesters, then The World is summer vacation. We've completed a cycle, the karmic pattern is over, and here we enjoy the freedom, consciousness, success and satisfaction that we worked our ass off for.

More than likely, we don't know how to accept The World's invitation to chill and bliss out. Is this a trap? There must be something left to do. *Checks phone. Reviews calendar.* Is it really safe to let go? We long for a break and then we get one and don't know what to do with ourselves. We book vacations and work through them, or aren't present because we're on our phone or behind a camera lens. Accept the break, you crazy person. This is a vital time for reflection and integration.

The journey was long, challenging and sometimes treacherous, but now we're home. We've arrived, and it feels right, even if it wasn't the destination we initially had in mind or thought we wanted. The World's vantage point offers a clear view of the perfection in each ostensible misstep, mistake, struggle and wrong turn. The product of this hindsight is both a sense of accomplishment and an awestruck humility at the immaculate workings of the universe.

While The World is the last card in the Major Arcana, it is not the endgame. We yearn for the wholeness and peace that it offers us, wax sentimental about a blank calendar and an empty inbox. And here we get it. We can stay here for a little while. Sometimes a day, or a week, and very occasionally we are welcome into this oasis for a couple of months. Sometimes it's as simple and brief as snuggling on your couch at the end of a long, productive day. It can come to us in the form of a specific event—leaving a job on great terms, or graduating from school or finishing a book.

The World will lead back to The Fool. We can't help ourselves. Energy festers if left to stagnate. We cannot be on vacation forever, nor do we truly want that. There will come a time where we again crave the wild journey, the mystery of the next step. We will go back into The Fool a little older, a little wiser, a little more equipped. We'll long for The World when we're tested by The Wheel of Fortune, in the throes of Death, shaken to our core by The Tower. But there will be a small, quiet part of us that will smile knowingly at the longing, all the while savoring every moment of this life's dazzling messiness.

Anecdote

The month before I moved to North Carolina was extremely chaotic. As my time in Brooklyn wound down, it all hit me at once. I was a tarot reader. I was moving to the South. There were so many unexpected twists and turns that, while they were all beautiful and perfect, I was still reeling from. I had just published an article in a major media outlet that brought an influx of new clients, in addition to trying to fit in the old-timers who wanted readings before I moved. My identity was stolen and over $10,000 worth of shit was purchased in my name. The packing process was tedious and unending. And more than that, leaving the city that gave me so much—that I experienced magic in, where I found such an amazing community—was breaking my heart.

I decided when we moved to Durham that I would not work for the first month. I had enough saved to justify it and hadn't taken any kind of break or vacation since I quit my job to become a full-time reader a year and a half before. It felt important, settling into a new home, to take space and process that wild and miraculous ride.

That first month, I made our house beautiful. I spent days in vintage and antique stores finding the perfect pieces for corners and hallways. I took long meandering walks around the city with Zadie and talked to strangers. I read books. I looked up recipes in the morning, went to the farmers' market to get ingredients and spent the entire day cooking a meal from scratch. I contacted friends I had fallen out of touch with. I went to the woods. I lounged in bed all day. I remembered things I enjoyed doing that got lost in the hustle. I felt proud of myself, grateful, humbled and awestruck by the journey that led me here, to this house in a city that, up until a couple years ago, I'd never heard of. I knew the month would end. I knew I was going to open Everyday Magic. I knew there was a whole new chapter of magical madness ahead. But for that month, it was time to rest.

In a Reading

The experience of wholeness. A happy ending, or satisfying outcome. Completion. Giving to yourself. Reflecting on what you've done. Earned retreat. Being rewarded. Realization. Success. Feeling content. There is nothing more to do at this moment but rest. Arriving home after a long journey. Connection to source.

THE
MINOR ARCANA

The four suits of the Minor Arcana comprise the majority of the cards in a tarot deck, but do not carry the same heavy-hitting lessons or staying power as the Majors. They are the details of life, the specific circumstances, the passing moments and fleeting situations. While these cards do not possess the same profundity as their Major counterpart, they are not trivial. They are the realities of living, the daily endeavor of being human. If the Major Arcana are the vital organs, then the Minor Arcana are the circulatory system that carries blood and oxygen throughout the body.

Starting at the Ace—the commencement, or invitation to begin the journey of that particular suit—and ending at the Ten—the saturation point, or apex of that suit's potential—the Minor Arcana are simpler energies to understand. In a reading, do not overthink their messages. It could be as simple as "he's an asshole" or "this conflict isn't worth spending too much time on because it will be over in three days." If the tarot is a mirror of our reality, then miring everything with dense meaning is not useful, necessary or accurate. Again, intuition is key here.

Numerologists have drawn parallels between each number, but it has never rung true to me, and trying to connect each number across suits has resulted in more confusion than clarity. The most intuitive through lines in each suit can be seen in the Aces, Fives and Tens.

Aces are tiny, beautifully wrapped gifts. Depending on where we're standing, we may not even see them, let alone consider picking them up. They are the babies of The Fool and The Magician, offering new beginnings and embodying the pure potential of the suits they correspond to. They do not possess the soul-level longing we feel to jump into the unknown when we meet The Fool, or the urgent action The Magician catalyzes. They are invitations into the journey of the Minor Arcana, and we do not always accept them. For every road we travel, there are a million paths we leave unexplored. Each Ace is a possibility. They let you know there is an opening. Trust yourself—it is not always possible to say yes to all of them. Make the decision you can live with.

Fives are the middle point of each suit, and the teen angst is so real here. Soon we will blossom into beautiful butterflies, but the transition is just fucking awkward. You're uncomfortable. You're angry and aggressive and sad and self-destructive. Your body is doing weird things and no one gets you. The easiest way to connect the Fives is to remember they all suck. Take the worst part of a suit's characteristics, add in puberty, growing pains and Emo music and you arrive at the Fives.

Tens are the saturation point of a card's potential, which can be either a pinnacle or an overdose depending on the suit. The two difficult Tens are the Wands and Swords—the product of too much action and too much thinking, respectively. The two happy Tens are the Cups and Pentacles—too much love and too much money. Where do I sign up? But hey, no light card is without its shadow and no difficult card without its silver lining—and regardless of the palatability of any of the Tens, they bring the suit to a close. This too shall pass, whether we like it or not.

THE SUIT OF WANDS

fire / spring / dawn / days

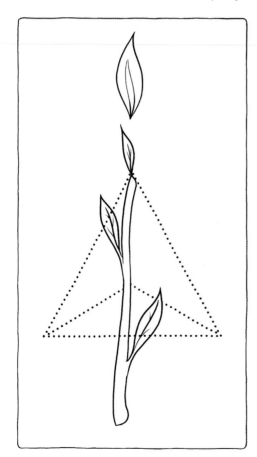

Wands represent action, passion, creativity, sexuality and movement in the world. They are the youngest suit of the tarot, and this youthful energy permeates the trajectory of the Wands. From new creative endeavors to exciting partnerships to fiery conflicts to overwhelming ourselves with taking too much on, the Wands carry us though the path of fire.

Ace of Wands—It's Lit

If the Ace cards offer beginnings, then the Ace of Wands presents us with a spark. A new passion, or budding inspiration. The presentation of a new creative outlet—fragile in its newness but warming in its light. It is potential energy that, if nurtured properly, becomes kinetic through the journey of Wands. The opportunity could be anything that embodies fire—creativity, passion, sexuality or leadership—and the prospect of it excites us. The enthusiasm this card brings with it cannot be faked or manufactured. Oftentimes there is not yet enough information available to assess the pros and cons of this new path, but, fuck, we still want to do it. We're buzzing to do it. It can be hard to imagine saying no to the Ace of Wands, even if it's not a fully informed decision. This card brings with it an overall feeling of revitalization and health and speaks to the powerful medicine of passion. I've seen this card show up alongside something ending, or when considering letting something go. Amid the loss, insecurity and uncertainty there is something else—lightness—something being born that is new and possible and yours. The Ace of Wands is the discovery of possibility.

Reinforced by: The Fool, The Magician, Ace of Pentacles, Eight of Pentacles

Opposed by: The Wheel of Fortune, Death, Two of Swords, Eight of Swords

Two of Wands—Let's Do the Damn Thing

In the Two of Wands, we harness the spark of the Ace and put it into action. We've shown it to someone and were met with an "oh my god, yes!" Excitement grows when it's shared, and in being seen we feel fortified and validated. Any insecurity about this new venture is soothed by the plans we make to act on it. In this card, we may feel energized by another person, and it can speak to a meaningful but short-lived connection. Maybe it is a twin flame, but not a soul mate. Or maybe you are strongly connected to another by a shared goal. The two wands in this card serve to mirror each other, and the reflection allows for both parties to point all their efforts in one direction. A strong and equal creative partnership can be indicated in the Two of Wands, which is both a lot of fun and increases manifestation potential. Like any of the Twos, this card can also present us with choice; in the spirit of fire, it encourages fearlessness in our decision.

Reinforced by: The Lovers, The Chariot, Two of Cups, Three of Pentacles

Opposed by: The High Priestess, The Hermit, Eight of Swords, Seven of Pentacles

Three of Wands—Looking Ahead

You are standing in the middle of something that you've made, and it's good. You did a thing. There's beauty inside of it. And yet, you kind of want to take a sledgehammer to the edges of it to make room for more. The Three of Wands allows us to see what something can become. The desire for expansion this card brings with it is not connected to selfishness or greed or ego—it is born of a transformative desire that is distinctly divine. In readings, I see this card connected to flashes of clarity or clairvoyance; where, for a moment, space and time fold in on themselves and allow us to glimpse something more. It is also the time to re-examine plans we've made that we cannot visualize coming to pass. "I just can't see it" has merit here. In the Three of Wands there is a strong possibility we've outgrown something. Do not postpone renovating your house for fear of the temporary disarray of construction. This is not a time for complacency. Follow your desire to lean into the unknown. Inversely, take time to appreciate what you've manifested so far. While having a corporate job wasn't my ultimate path, I needed to first get that job in order to realize I didn't want it. Do not diminish the thing you've outgrown, because it was that very thing that allowed you to grow and then outgrow in the first place.

Reinforced by: The Hanged Man, The Tower, Seven of Wands, Nine of Pentacles
Opposed by: The Devil, Two of Swords, Eight of Swords, Four of Pentacles

Four of Wands—Work Hard Play Hard

Time to turn up. Four is a number that typically represents structure (The Emperor is Arcanum IV), but when you blend the stability of this number with the fiery nature of the Wands, you just get a really well-planned party. Representing celebrations of all sorts, you can breathe a sigh of relief when this card shows up in a reading. We've made something beautiful, and it's time to gather with the people we love and feel really fucking good about that. It could be celebrating a strong and meaningful relationship in the form of a wedding, or the birthday party of a friend you love. Since Everyday Magic opened, it has expanded in beautiful, unexpected ways. We have two employees, an in-house herbalist and a plant shop renting out the back space—a squad made up of the most intelligent, intuitive, hardworking and straight-up cool women I have ever met. We just had a holiday dinner together after nine months of tending to and growing this space, and the feelings of love, gratitude and respect we all have for each other lit up the whole evening. The champagne didn't hurt, either.

Reinforced by: The Emperor, The Sun, The World, Three of Cups
Opposed by: The Hermit, The Tower, Five of Wands, Eight of Cups

Five of Wands—Wait, Why Are We Even Fighting?

Maybe you turned up too hard in the Four of Wands, and maybe now it's the end of the night and you're belligerent and trying to start some shit. You're kinda pissed, kinda looking for a fight, kinda trying to break something just to produce loud sounds and kick up dust. We've all been here, when our partner comes home a little late from an innocent outing and we are faced with the choice of letting it go or turning the conversation into a "you always do this" blowout for the gods. The Five of Wands is unfocused, superficial conflict. The arguing, chaos and anger are to no end. Maybe you're right, but being right doesn't really matter. I've had fights like these with friends, cracking up laughing mid-argument in spite of ourselves. Try not to hold on to or get sucked into this drama. It's not yours, or at least it doesn't have to be. Maybe anger is being used to hide a secondary emotion—hurt or vulnerability. Re-assess the conflict in your life and the value of furthering it. There are battles worth fighting; is this one of them? Even if you end up being right, will it feel like you won?

Reinforced by: The Tower, Eight of Wands, Seven of Wands, Five of Swords

Opposed by: Strength, The Hanged Man, Four of Swords, Nine of Cups

Six of Wands—When They Go Low, We Go High

You've made it out of a scuffle safely and better. Fresh from battle, maybe the victory hasn't set in yet. But soon you will see that the drama is over, your integrity is intact and your sense of self is fortified as a result of your experience. This card shows up in a reading to let clients reflect on their own goodness and strength. Against the odds, they did right by themselves. Explore the possibility that you are not broken. Maybe, in spite of everything and because of everything, you are miraculously, perfectly whole. The circumstances have only strengthened your heart and cleared your voice. The power of the Six of Wands resides in acknowledging all the different ways a situation could have been handled— cracking under pressure, succumbing to negativity, losing yourself in drama—and appreciating yourself for choosing a higher road.

Reinforced by: Strength, Temperance, Four of Swords, Six of Swords

Opposed by: Five of Wands, Seven of Swords, Five of Cups, Five of Pentacles

Seven of Wands—Come At Me Bro

With strengthened convictions and a feeling of having something to protect, we are ready to fight for what we believe in—but do we need to? It can be lonely at the top, and the Seven of Wands cautions us to resist aggression and paranoia. Being secure in who we are and what we stand for is paramount to responsibly using the Seven of Wands. A strong sense of self allows us to correctly perceive toxic energies, ill-wishers, jealousy or unhealthy competition. If this is the case, the Seven of Wands allows us to walk away or fight if we have to. Most commonly, I see this card show up as external influences that no longer support the client's highest intention. Here, courage is called for. Whether or not there is still a connection to it, it is time to keep going, and sometimes that means leaving things behind.

Reinforced by: Justice, Ace of Swords, Eight of Cups, Four of Pentacles

Opposed by: The Hanged Man, Nine of Pentacles, Ten of Pentacles, Ten of Cups

Eight of Wands—Married to the Hustle

The rapid-fire movement of the Eight of Wands is both an exciting and all-consuming time. True to the wand's swiftness, this card enters quickly and demands quickness on the part of its recipient. One after another, we are presented with opportunities that demand our full attention and creativity, and we want to give it our all. With these opportunities, the prospects of success, travel and adventure are introduced. A good omen for people looking for jobs or searching for a new path, this is not a time for indecision or settling. It can also threaten long-standing commitments that, while necessary, are not as exciting as the Eight of Wands. People consumed with this energy can be horrible company because they are entirely focused on a goal and neglecting other aspects of life. Unless this is a chronic behavioral pattern, encourage patience—oftentimes the Eight of Wands leaves as quickly as it came.

Reinforced by: The Magician, The Chariot, The Tower, The Wheel of Fortune

Opposed by: The High Priestess, The Hermit, Seven of Cups, Eight of Pentacles

Nine of Wands—You Got This

A lot has been demanded of you to get this far, and you're tired. Whatever unexpected, glittery, wooded moonlit path you're walking has tested your endurance, but you're almost there. Maybe the next step is uncertain, or maybe the next step seems like a rickety, structurally unsound piece of shit step that you don't feel like scaling anyway. Maybe you can't see the step after the one in front of you. Maybe no one gave you a map. Maybe you don't know where the hell you're going. Maybe it's dark out. Maybe, in moments of weakness, you long to go back. But there is no going back, you already know that, and if you're being honest with yourself you don't want to. The fulfillment, inspiration and purpose you crave are awaiting you. Grumble all you want, but you were never going to say no to this journey. Accept where you are, rest if you need to and then get your ass up and keep going.

Reinforced by: The Fool, The Star, The Moon, Ace of Wands

Opposed by: The Sun, Ace of Swords, Eight of Cups, Seven of Pentacles

Ten of Wands—Let It Be

You have taken on too much fire, without enough oxygen to feed it, and you're literally burnt out. In the Ten of Wands, we are overwhelmed, overburdened and just generally over it. While all the responsibilities we have taken on may be good ones, there are just too many of them. The result is that, even if we see success, we don't care. We won't celebrate it because we're too busy, or can't feel it because we're so energetically depleted. You are not fully useful to any cause because you have spread yourself too thin. It is time to simplify. It is time to let go of some things. It may be time to walk away from an unsolvable situation. Use your discernment in deciding what needs to go, but know that there is no negotiating the fact that when the Ten of Wands appears, you must pare down.

Reinforced by: The Hermit, Justice, Death, Ten of Swords

Opposed by: The Empress, Temperance, Two of Pentacles, Eight of Pentacles

THE SUIT OF SWORDS
air / winter / night / weeks

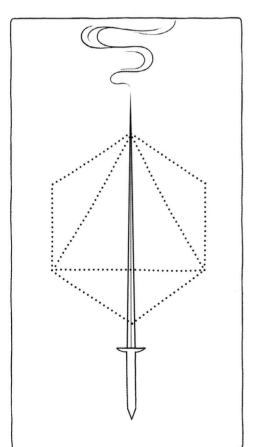

Swords are thoughts, fears, intellect, conflict and the analytical mind. This is where I adopt a dramatic, deep voice and say something like "the mind is a powerful and terrible thing" or something equally trite. Like a weapon, the sharpness of our minds can cut through the old, the superfluous and that which no longer serves. It can also cause harm to ourselves and others if used improperly or with malice. The journey of Swords is fraught with difficulty and blockages, with mental statements, betrayal, naivety and self-harm all lurking within this tricky suit. However, the Swords also provide lovely experiences, such as moments of clarity or a long-awaited, new idea.

Ace of Swords—I Have An Idea

With the Ace cards bringing new opportunity, and the suit of Swords representing intellect and cognitive function, it stands to reason that when the Ace of Swords appears in a reading it offers us a new way to use our minds. An epiphany, idea or different approach on how to handle a situation is common. The Ace of Swords aids in clear communication on all fronts, but is especially useful for writing. While most of the Swords cards carry a negative or positive connotation, the Ace represents total neutrality. This card almost buzzes with the infinite potential of a sharp mind. It begs the question, why possess a weapon like this? It may be wielded to perpetuate manipulation, dishonesty and personal gain. But pursuing truth, enforcing justice and maintaining balance are just as possible. If this card could speak it may say, "Congratulations, you're not an idiot. Now don't be an asshole."

Reinforced by: Justice, The Sun, Two of Wands, Three of Pentacles

Opposed by: The Moon, Two of Swords, Four of Swords, Seven of Cups

Two of Swords—I Can't Even

But you can though, you know? While the blockage we encounter in the Two of Swords feels very real, it is just a low-level mental block, easily solved by pulling your head out of your ass. That annoying cliché about our thoughts becoming our reality is relevant here, and whatever physical discomfort brought with the Two of Swords can be traced back to mental stagnation or an unwillingness to acknowledge the truth. Most often, this card causes issues in the sacral chakra, suppressing sexual and creative expression. Whatever the bind is, we put ourselves there, and only we can get ourselves out of it. This is when your friends get annoyed with you because you keep asking for advice you don't take, lamenting your predicament while simultaneously keeping yourself mired in its grasp. While the Two of Swords often represents a stalemate, it can also indicate a ceasefire. It may be time to retreat from action. Take a break from agonizing over a decision or trying to force an outcome until more information is available.

Reinforced by: The High Priestess, The Hanged Man, The Devil, Eight of Swords

Opposed by: Strength, The Sun, Ace of Wands, Five of Wands

Three of Swords—The First Cut Is the Deepest

Searing, immediate, overwhelming pain characterizes this infamous card. Traditionally depicted as a heart pierced by three swords, the experience of the Three of Swords is always difficult. Not only are we feeling extreme heartache, but it is typically at the hands of people we trusted. Being cheated on, backstabbed, disappointed and undermined could all bring about the acute distress of the Three of Swords. The wreckage of this card is not in the transgression itself, but rather the discovery of it. The shattering aftermath of being wronged can feel like an unending nightmare, and there is little that can be done for people going through it. It will not feel like this forever. You will get through it and feel differently even if you can't imagine either happening in this moment. You will share your story with someone else at some point, and it will help them to feel less alone, and then and only then will you understand why you had to endure all that shittiness. But until then, it just fucking sucks, and no one and nothing but time is going to make it better.

Reinforced by: The Tower, Seven of Swords, Five of Cups, Seven of Cups

Opposed by: The Magician, The Sun, Judgment, Ace of Swords

Four of Swords—Take a Disco Nap

The Four of Swords calls us to lay down our arms. It's time for some R&R—get a massage, binge-watch a Netflix series, take a quick nap. In most depictions of this card, the Swords are not being used. They are hung up above the person, or in an otherwise inactive state. In the midst of a suit as heavy and problematic as the Swords, it may feel counterintuitive to go unarmed in this environment, but they are truly not needed here. The Four of Swords signifies intellectual maturity, a by-product of which is knowing when vulnerability and surrender are more productive than argument and debate. With a stable and organized mental body, we are able to mindfully respond to the world around us rather than being chained to our reactions. Find your center. Being steady and fearless even though there may be reasons fear is called for here. Sometimes, the most effective way to disarm a situation is to show someone your heart, and therein lies the wisdom of the Four of Swords.

Reinforced by: The Empress, Strength, Six of Wands, Ten of Cups

Opposed by: Five of Wands, Seven of Wands, Five of Swords, Son of Swords

Five of Swords—Check Yourself before You Wreck Yourself

The first thing I ask people when the Five of Swords appears is if they would ever, in a million years, treat someone else the way they are treating themselves right now. No matter how much of a stone cold asshole they are, the answer is always no. This card speaks to the cruel, cutting and downright twisted ways that we abuse ourselves. The voice that constantly reminds us that, no matter how hard we try, we will always be a worthless piece of shit, and we've somehow managed to fool anyone who thinks otherwise. The Five of Swords lets us know we are in an unproductive and oftentimes dangerous loop of self-harm. There is nothing to be gained by remaining here. Show yourself mercy, ask for help and move on.

Reinforced by: The Wheel of Fortune, The Devil, Nine of Swords, Ten of Swords

Opposed by: The Empress, Judgment, Ace of Cups, Six of Wands

Six of Swords—Ghosting the Haters

Maybe the situation isn't resolved, maybe it still stings, maybe you haven't fully recovered—but it's still time to bounce. Not every ending comes with a neat bow and a sense of closure. Sometimes there is wisdom in giving up, and this is one of those times. We are not ghosting because we don't wanna deal, but rather because we cannot stay in this environment without continuing to hurt ourselves. The Six of Swords calls us to move away from the past with the promise of clarity and abundance ahead—and in this card we are already on the way out. We are no longer stuck with the haters, nor are we standing victoriously on the other side. Disarming the Swords' ability to harm us is the task of this card, and sometimes that means dropping them altogether. While lightness and relief may accompany abandoning the weight, the transition the Six of Swords facilitates is not without sacrifice. There was a period of years where I did not speak to anyone in my family. To stay in a relationship with them was destroying me, I didn't doubt that this was a decision I needed to make for myself, but it also meant wrestling with impossible, shame-inducing questions about my duty as a daughter and a sister. Oftentimes this card will show up as a sign of travel, or taking physical distance in order to gain perspective. Another possibility of the Six of Swords is the achievement of mental harmony and experiencing delight at the fruits of our intellect.

Reinforced by: The Hanged Man, Death, Ten of Wands, Eight of Cups

Opposed by: The Chariot, The Lovers, Four of Pentacles, Nine of Pentacles

Seven of Swords—Why the Fuck You Lyin'?

When the Seven of Swords is pulled in a reading, either you are being dishonest or someone is being dishonest with you. This card is a bummer. Not only are you lying, you know you're lying and trying to make it look like you're not. Dude, come on. Are you trying to protect yourself? Are you trying to avoid getting into trouble? It honestly doesn't matter why. You're being the worst, and when the truth comes out someone is going to get hurt. Speaking to deception, secrets and trickery—we are asked to examine our motivations here to determine if it is really worth continuing on this way. Why are we engaging in a behavior that we must hide? Rarely does a healthy, positive activity call for this kind of sneaking around. More often, antics like these are used by addicts and cheaters. Perhaps there is a reason to not share your goings-on with others, but this card asks us to make damn sure that the reasoning for concealing information is ethically sound. Sometimes this card can point to a person being dishonest with themselves, or withholding something for the sake of self-protection. Again, examining the necessity of this is called for here. If you're in a situation where you don't feel safe being honest, it may be the time to change your circumstances.

Reinforced by: The Devil, The Moon, Three of Swords, Seven of Cups

Opposed by: The Hierophant, The Sun, Six of Wands, Ace of Swords

Eight of Swords—It Doesn't Have to Be This Hard

The Eight of Swords speaks to a fear-based paralysis that can translate to others as laziness. It is difficult to be around people in this energy because of their seeming refusal to pull themselves up by their bootstraps and help themselves. However, the perceived threats of moving forward seem very real in the Eight of Swords, often triggering feelings of helplessness and being stuck that predate the current situation. While this means that the perceived dangers aren't real, it does little to heal the deep-seated victimization that this card brings to the surface. A damaged thought process brought us to this place, so it is safe to conclude that more thinking will not solve this predicament. Small steps, methodical action and setting short-term goals will, over time, reverse the self-imposed bondage of this card.

Reinforced by: Two of Swords, Nine of Swords, Eight of Cups, Four of Pentacles

Opposed by: The Magician, The Chariot, Eight of Wands, Seven of Pentacles

Nine of Swords—I'm Literally Having a Panic Attack

One of the most dark and bizarre cards of the tarot, the Nine of Swords has been interpreted with various levels of severity. While the sensation of this card is unpleasant, I don't view it as the dark night of the soul it is sometimes described as. Tensions are high, anxiety is on fleek and stress levels are off the charts, but this card usually presents itself in readings as a sort of detox. The cause of this worry is coursing through, and eventually out, of our system, and we are better off without it, even if the process of clearing it is gross and gnarly. No one enjoys throwing up, but most people will agree that they are better off expelling whatever is making them sick. This card can manifest as insomnia or nightmares, insane thoughts or feelings of disquiet that are not necessarily tied to the present moment. Perhaps old toxins are resurfacing, possibly for the sake of being cleared. That does not diminish the intensity of the Nine of Swords, but it does help inform what is often a weird and painful experience. Let it run its course, because it will, and in the meantime consider seeking extra support and try to remember that your thoughts do not define you.

Reinforced by: The Devil, The Moon, Eight of Swords, Ten of Swords

Opposed by: The Hierophant, The Sun, Ace of Cups, Nine of Cups

Ten of Swords—I'm Dead

How can you be dead? You're still breathing. Your brain is formulating the thought that you're dead. Well, it's settled, you're not dead. Shit sucks, you're at an all-time low, but you are unequivocally still alive. Now, where are we? Looking around, I'd say we're at the bottom. You've failed to heed the warnings of the earlier Swords, instead charging ahead in your victimization, self-sabotage and dishonesty, and have eviscerated yourself in the process. You murdered yourself with your thoughts. Are you done yet? Maybe I sound harsh, but the good news about my unforgiving attitude toward this card is that things aren't as bad as they seem.

With the Swords, only you can turn things around, and maybe it didn't seem bad enough to acknowledge the necessity of doing so until now. It can be humiliating to accept we've done this to ourselves, but to do so is the first step toward meaningful change. All the advice you didn't take, help you didn't ask for, support you didn't seek out—get on that. This is the end of something, but it's not the end of you. Cut your losses, learn from your mistakes and accept the bitter but crucial lesson of humility this card teaches us. There's nowhere to go but up, my friend.

Reinforced by: Death, Ten of Wands, Nine of Swords, Five of Pentacles

Opposed by: The Chariot, The World, Three of Wands, Six of Pentacles

THE SUIT OF CUPS
water / summer / daytime / months

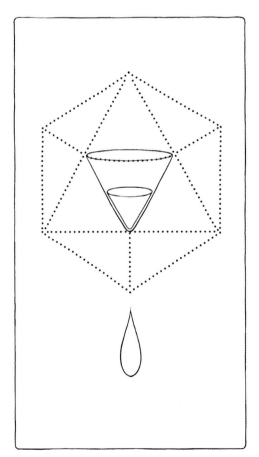

The suit of Cups embodies emotions, love, healing, fulfillment and romance, and the journey of the suit encompasses the experiences of our emotional landscape. Spanning from the enjoyable—new romance, strong friendships, community, nostalgia—to the profound—birth, grief, loss and healing—to the challenging—trauma, selfishness, uncertainty and deceit. The Cups ask us to go inside and take stock; they are an invitation to know ourselves better and, consequentially, connect more authentically with others.

Ace of Cups—What if I'm Actually Gorgeous?
A sweet card of self-love and renewal, the Ace of Cups offers us some much-needed hydration after the draining and sometimes futile expedition of the Swords. A suit of nourishment, healing, love and spirituality—the Ace gives us the initial taste of the Cups' qualities, and with it, hope. In this period of peace, we are urged to look inside and connect with our real needs. The Swords unearthed the wounded, undeveloped aspects of our psyche, and here we

enact the self-care needed to heal. This is the appropriate time to bring in a healer or support system, or to consider training in a healing modality. The Ace of Cups is a calling to more deeply explore the nature of our emotional landscape and often shows up alongside spiritual experiences, birth and fertility and viewing ourselves in a more forgiving light. While the Ace of Cups does not signify a romantic relationship, it establishes the foundation needed to cultivate healthy connections with others.

Reinforced by: The Empress, The Hierophant, The Hermit, The Star

Opposed by: The Wheel of Fortune, The Emperor, Five of Swords, Five of Cups

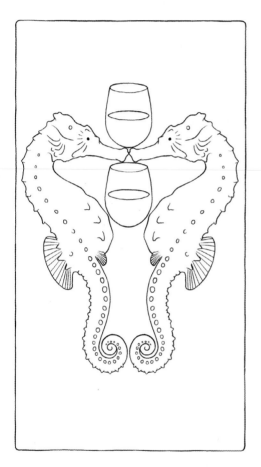

Two of Cups—An Amazing Tinder Date

The baby of The Lovers card, the Two of Cups shows a promising new connection, typically of the romantic variety. It can reflect a first date that went unbelievably well, or the giddiness that accompanies a new relationship where the other person hasn't done anything to make you hate them yet. Dating can be a challenging and awkward endeavor, and while my clients come to me with all kinds of questions, they are at their most exposed when asking about romantic relationships. This card is reassurance. You are in a good situation. Both parties have something to offer each other that may be different in content but equal in value. What is more, they want to give to each other. No insecurity-inducing games, no excuses. Maybe it is too soon to tell if this is a soul mate, future life partner, person you will die with—but reaching for those answers comes from a place of fear, anyway. Right now, the answer is yes. This is right. It's new and possesses the formalities and mysteries of a new relationship, but the joy of discovery and intimacy of the Two of Cups is not to be missed. It is falling in love. We live for this.

Reinforced by: The Lovers, Two of Wands, Nine of Cups, Nine of Pentacles

Opposed by: The Hermit, The Devil, Seven of Cups, Eight of Cups

Three of Cups—The Girl Gang

When the squad gets together we enter into the warm, content, glittery cocoon of the Three of Cups. Who do you love the most? Who do you get together with and feel like all is right, like nothing is missing, like the world could end right then and it would be sort of fine? Whether you are turning up, staying in, working, devastated, experiencing a crisis or doing nothing—it is better and easier simply because these people are with you. A card that speaks to a soul-level connection between people, it shows up to tell us we are surrounded by people who have our back, who want to show up for us, who will be there through thick and thin. Let them in. Allow the nourishment that can be delivered only by true friendship. Fully accepting love can be an emotional and scary endeavor, but if there was ever a time to experiment with it, it is here with these people. Have fun, feel blessed, you are never alone if you don't choose to be.

Reinforced by: The Empress, Four of Wands, Three of Pentacles, Nine of Pentacles
Opposed by: The Hermit, The Hanged Man, Four of Cups, Five of Pentacles

Four of Cups—You're Being a Brat

You are surrounded by emotional abundance, support and sustenance that you refuse to see. Rather, you are focusing on what you don't have. The Four of Cups is a consuming energy of petty fear. Scarcity, lack and selfishness characterize this alienating card—and while no one outright enjoys feeling alone or being small, there is a self-righteous, negative pleasure derived from the idea that no one gets it. Nothing drains a relationship faster than lack of generosity, and this card is a gentle urging to look around and gain some perspective. The not-so-gentle message is to stop being a brat, but this is information that must be intuitively delivered in varying degrees of bluntness depending on the client. Inversely, if you are a person who gives too much, the Four of Cups can represent being protective of your emotional energy, taking care of yourself before you take care of others and setting boundaries.

Reinforced by: The Hermit, Two of Swords, Four of Pentacles, Five of Pentacles
Opposed by: The Lovers, Three of Cups, Nine of Cups, Ten of Cups

Five of Cups—Teen Angst (and Real Angst)

Caused by a disappointment, death or things not going as planned, the Five of Cups is an indication of grief. Rather than the acute and immediate response depicted in the Three of Swords, this card speaks to residual sadness and the inability to move on. While it may point to a recent loss, it can also reveal a hurt that was never properly processed. All of the five cards possess an adolescent quality; as the suit's middle point, this card may excavate old wounds that call for inner-child healing. When a client faces this card, be gentle. You may be reading for a fully functioning adult, but there is a strong possibility that in this place they are transported back to an injured, younger version of themselves. Maybe, at whatever age the wound was inflicted, it wasn't safe to grieve, or they didn't know how, but now is the time to feel it. The continued denial of this experience translates into self-pity, blame and depression. This can pass, but there are no cheats here; we cannot disappear painful emotions. The gift of the Five of Cups is that it presents an opportunity to feel our heart, even when it is heavy and broken, and there is beauty in that. The only way out is through.

Reinforced by: Death, The Tower, Three of Swords, Six of Cups

Opposed by: The Fool, The Sun, The World, Ten of Cups

Six of Cups—The Emotionally Manipulative Movie Montage

Bouts of nostalgia and sentimentality often accompany the sweet energy of the Six of Cups. Specifically correlating to childhood, this card brings up the matters of home, family and where we came from. While the Six cards are thought to display a harmonious implementation of a suit's characteristics, I grew up in a chaotic shit show, and the weepy, affectionate feeling of this card is lost on me. The only through line of this card, in my experience, is that it asks to look back. What hindsight reveals is as different and varied as there are people's pasts. It is not uncommon for the Six of Cups to speak to family karma, shadow inheritance and ancestral baggage. Either way, there is something to gain by reflecting on the past. Whether it is a smell that brings you back to your grandmother's kitchen, feeling comforted by moments in your youth or facing unresolved issues, the Six of Cups is an invitation to remember.

Reinforced by: The Wheel of Fortune, Five of Cups, Nine of Pentacles, the Court Cards as family members

Opposed by: The Emperor, Three of Wands, Ace of Swords, Two of Swords

Seven of Cups—The Indecisive Softboy

The alternate title for this ungrounded, dreamlike energy is, "I think the acid just kicked in." The experience of the Seven of Cups is that of having multiple layers of skin peeled off—unburdened of ego, we are overwhelmed by the beauty of the world. It is a visceral sensation of love, appreciation and affection. But it's also kind of like hearing colors or tasting sound, if you know what I'm saying. It is difficult to trust yourself or other people in this energy, as things are often not as they seem. I think of the Seven of Cups as walking into a carnival funhouse full of smoke and mirrors, which is only a place you want to be in like, maybe .01% of the time. There is a nagging feeling that the emotionality of the Seven of Cups is self-serving, or otherwise manufactured. Think: drunk nights where you really, really love everyone so much, or when you're tripping and are brought to tears by a tree because it's so wise and stoic and just, like, knows. The surrender of the Seven of Cups can be an antidote for taking yourself too seriously or not stopping to smell the roses. It can be fodder for imagination and inspiration. But, more often than not, it is indicative of a problem. At

best, you are indecisive, non-committal and identify a little too strongly with Drake songs. At worst, you are flirting with addiction, escapism and retreating into a strong fantasy life. This is not a mind-set conducive to clarity or decisive action. Consider the ways in which you are delaying reality, at what cost and at whose expense. Most likely, it is time to get grounded.

Reinforced by: The Devil, The Moon, Seven of Swords, Nine of Cups

Opposed by: The High Priestess, Justice, Temperance, Ace of Swords

Eight of Cups—The Shitty Breakup

Similar to the Six of Swords, Six of Wands and Seven of Wands, the Eight of Cups revisits the idea of letting go of something that isn't serving us. So what differentiates this card from others that hold comparable meanings? In the Wands and Swords, there is a desire to let go, and the act of doing so brings with it some immediate sense of freedom and release. While it may not have been easy, there was an undeniable rightness to it. Not so in the Eight of Cups. The broken relationship, behavior or situation depicted here leaves us heartbroken, devastated and laid bare. The red flags, the moments of clarity and the invitations to let go before it reached this point were ignored. We couldn't or wouldn't, and here we are, still holding on trying to repair this broken thing. But the shards of it are slicing open the pads of our fingertips, already scarred from picking up the same sharp pieces over and over again. I imagine the soldiers who fought in Vietnam, maimed and traumatized and killed in a war they were never going to win, felt something similar to the Eight of Cups. There is nothing left for you here. Put the ruins behind you. Solace will come eventually, because a relationship with faith is born in these times when there is nothing and no one else to reach for. This will fundamentally alter the treatment you are willing to accept. In time, it will restructure your priorities, values and boundaries. But right now you have to stop the bleeding. Run, walk, limp or crawl—but it's time to go.

Reinforced by: The Hermit, The Tower, Six of Swords, Ten of Swords
Opposed by: The Devil, The Wheel of Fortune, Two of Swords, Five of Cups

Nine of Cups—Blissed Out

The most obvious meaning of this happy card is fertility, gestation and pregnancy, both in the literal and metaphorical sense. I honestly don't have much to say when the Nine of Cups is drawn in a reading except to embrace it. You are in a period of contentment, joy and comfort. Like movies, readings are less interesting when all is well. You found everything you didn't know you were looking for when you left the wreckage of the Eight, and it's sublime. Life is good, fam. Not to interrupt your bliss—but the Nine of Cups also contains the faintest whisper of a warning: Things are always ripest right before they rot. In extreme cases, it may insinuate numbness, overindulgence and even addiction. More often, the rot is due to smugness and self-satisfaction. Think: couples in their early twenties who drone on about how lucky they are to have found each other and, like, people wait their whole lives and never get to experience what they have together. Do not apologize for or downplay your blessings, but let it live alongside a gratitude and humility for the forces that brought you here. It wasn't without help, trial, heartache and periods of thinking you would never reach this point. Wear your happiness honestly and generously, and you are in for a lovely time.

Reinforced by: The Lovers, The World, Four of Swords, Nine of Pentacles
Opposed by: The Hermit, The Tower, Three of Swords, Five of Swords

Ten of Cups—A Powerful Beyoncé Music Video

The question we ask in the Ace of Cups, "What if I'm actually gorgeous?" is answered in the Ten with a resounding, "Hell yes you are, honey." This card is the apex of feminine power, and we're feelin' like a queen and a goddess, gentle and powerful, a nurturer and a warrior, fierce and soft, overflowing and full all at the same time. The dazzling, bright, hot stage lights inside us switched on, and we can finally bear witness to our own radiance and magnetism. Physicality has no bearing on the effects of this card; anyone embodying this energy is glowing from the inside out. There is no mistaking this glow. No amount of highlighter can make you this radiant, and the currency of it far outweighs aesthetic perfection. We know this. We sense it in others. We feel it course through our veins. The precarious happiness discovered in the Nine of Cups stabilizes and grounds in the Ten. In this place, we are in the best possible position to give to the world. Fortified by an understanding of our value and secure enough to ask for what we need, the Ten of Cups shows us perfect reciprocity, the gorgeous ripple effect of living a big life.

Reinforced by: The High Priestess, Judgment, Nine of Cups, Ten of Pentacles
Opposed by: The Hermit, Nine of Wands, Four of Cups, Four of Pentacles

THE SUIT OF PENTACLES
earth / autumn / dusk / years

Pentacles are the oldest suit in the tarot and thereby possess a stability earned through travelling through the first three suits of the tarot. They deal in the physical: work, money, health and home. Financial uncertainty and financial abundance, new ventures in work, building a family, long-term investment and perfecting a craft or trade are all aspects of life addressed in the Pentacles.

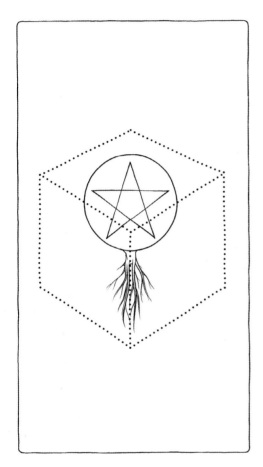

Ace of Pentacles—Progress Not Perfection

With Pentacles dealing in all things material, this Ace presents us with a seed. Oftentimes the gift of the Ace of Pentacles can be underwhelming, or not read as a gift at all. We wished for a fully blooming garden, and all we get is this crappy little seed? Patience, young grasshopper. The payoff of the Pentacles is not immediate, but the yield is sturdier and more reliable than anything produced by the preceding three suits. This is the long con, and even if it were possible to jump from beginning to end in a single breath, you would be cheating yourself out of so much by doing so. The Ace of Pentacles shows us both humble beginnings and unlimited potential. With patience, diligence and attentiveness, the seed blooms and transcends its initial form. It could be said that the entire journey of Pentacles is the story of how we care for the seed received in the Ace, so put on your overalls and grab your gardening equipment because it's time to get your hands dirty and work for what you want. Spanning the areas of money, career, health and home, this card can show a work opportunity that—while it may not be your dream job—is an improvement on the current sitch and a step toward your professional aspirations. Maybe you need an influx of cash to start a business or take a trip and your parents let you move back in, rent-free, to save money. Maybe you buy your first home knowing it's not perfect, or move to a city you know you don't want to live in forever, or buy your first car and it's a used Honda and not a new Audi. The dream job, booming business, incredible vacation, perfect home and shiny new car possess more meaning and produce more satisfaction because of what it took to get there. They are objects that hold heart and not vapid material trappings. This is the curse of the wealthy, the spoiled and the privileged who never learn the value of hard work. Life is a journey, not a destination, and while I hate myself for busting out that old cliché, try to enjoy the fucking journey, will ya?

Reinforced by: The Chariot, Three of Wands, Six of Pentacles, Eight of Pentacles
Opposed by: The High Priestess, The World, Eight of Swords, Ten of Pentacles

Two of Pentacles—Find You a Girl Who Can Do Both

A practical card, the Two of Pentacles speaks to juggling tasks, managing responsibilities and maintaining a work-life balance. I think we can all agree that being a human is hard. Forget dealing with our emotions or contemplating our spirituality or searching for higher meaning— the mere logistics of being a living, breathing person is complicated. There's a lot of paperwork, fine print and calendar management involved, and the Two of Pentacles speaks to keeping our shit together in this arena. In addition to balance, smooth transition is another theme of this card, or holding on to something you already have while switching over to something new. It can illustrate applying to jobs before you graduate, taking a bartending gig to support yourself while writing the next great American novel or going from boss bitch at work to bae at home. Lady in the streets, freak in the sheets kinda thing. A reminder to stay in our own lane because we have more than enough to keep us busy, the Two of Pentacles is a practice of healthy boundaries. The Two of Pentacles doesn't answer work e-mails after 7 p.m. and cleans its apartment every Sunday. Emotionality and personal attachment can make it difficult to assess and compartmentalize a situation from the rational lens of this card. While the Two of Pentacles is a card that makes logical sense, it is also an art form.

Reinforced by: Justice, Temperance, Ace of Swords, Seven of Pentacles
Opposed by: The Moon, Eight of Wands, Ten of Wands, Nine of Swords

Three of Pentacles—The Harry Potter Squad

Obviously I was going to find at least one card to cross-reference with Harry Potter, and this is it guys. The value of teamwork, knowing your strengths and weaknesses, and working with others to create something bigger than the sum of your parts is the essence of the Three of Pentacles. Harry, Ron and Hermione are all imperfect characters—what Harry lacks in book-smarts he makes up for in bravery; Ron is moody and insecure but has a knack for pinch-hitting; and Hermione repeatedly saves both of their asses with her encyclopedic mind, but also halts progress on account of her rigidity. Their humanity makes them lovable and relatable, but as individuals there is no story. Not even with Harry, who wouldn't have survived his first year at Hogwarts without his two friends. It is the union of these three people, their combined strength, that allowed them to accomplish the impossible. When the Three of Pentacles is pulled, it is time to build a team. Be honest in your self-evaluation to determine what kind of help is needed and thorough in your search for the right people. Success is within reach, but will not be achieved alone.

Reinforced by: The Lovers, Four of Wands, Three of Cups, Eight of Pentacles

Opposed by: The Hermit, Four of Pentacles, Two of Swords, Seven of Cups

Four of Pentacles—Your Stingy Friend

Where the Four of Cups shows emotional selfishness, the Four of Pentacles is physical stinginess. They are two peas in the same crappy pod and often show up together with similar messages: loosen your grip, soften your gaze and look around. The fear of not having enough is dictating your actions, and it is making you and everyone around you miserable. Scarcity and lack are illusions. When we subscribe to these myths, our vision narrows, paranoia kicks in and we become very small. In a twelve-step meeting a few years back I heard someone say, "If I have next to nothing, I need to give it away to get more," and I hear these words every time the Four of Pentacles is drawn in a reading. It could be the mantra that soothes the tension of this card. A lot of extraneous baggage has been globbed onto the concept of money—it is equated with worth, validity, happiness and a lot of other things that have nothing to do with it. Distilled into its simplest function, money is energy. A source we pull from that enables us to do things we want. It is a means to an end, even if that end is a sense of security. Some of the wealthiest people I know are crippled by fear of money, trapped in the Four of Pentacles long after there is any reason to have this mind-set. Before you justify this cheapness as being responsible, remember that the next card is one of poverty, destitution and illness. Greed and possessiveness do not translate to prudence. If money is energy, then in this card we block it, working directly against our own self-interests. You are holding on so tightly to what you have—even if it's not enough, even if it's not working—that you created a closed structure. There is no room for abundance until you chill the fuck out.

Reinforced by: The Devil, Seven of Wands, Four of Cups, Five of Pentacles

Opposed by: The Hanged Man, The Star, Four of Swords, Six of Pentacles

Five of Pentacles—Help Me, I'm Poor

In the last of the shitty Fives we fall on hard times. Sickness, depletion and financial difficulty are all possibilities when the Five of Pentacles appears in a reading, and the task of this card is to confront these unwelcome realities. You've squandered your resources, ignored the flashing gas light and neglected the seed given to you in the Ace. Your garden is barren, you plant killer! This is an uncomfortable, sometimes shameful thing to face. But you know what, it fucking happens. Accounts get overdrawn, boundaries get crossed, self-care gets delayed indefinitely. This is our body being like, "Dude, how long did you think you were going to get away with this shit?" Getting consumed by the seriousness of this card, even if it is serious, only feeds the problem. If speaking about a job, you are putting more into it than you are getting out of it and feeling drained as a result. In a relationship, you are malnourished. In a physical sense, your body isn't working the way it's supposed to. Regardless of where this deficiency is experienced, the common denominator of this card is feeling unsupported. So, um, support is the medicine to this, in case you needed me to spell it out real simple. Don't be a martyr.

Reinforced by: The Devil, Three of Swords, Five of Swords, Five of Cups

Opposed by: The Sun, Nine of Wands, Three of Cups, Three of Pentacles

Six of Pentacles—It's All Happening

After the famine of the Five of Pentacles we're determined to not let that shit happen again. We research fertilizer, seed strains, irrigation methods and all the other stuff that farmers and gardeners do. We plant our seeds lovingly and intentionally and commit to caring for them. And, holy shit, they all sprout up in beautiful little buds of possibility. We're not rich, but who cares? We're so in love with what we started, so dazzled by these miraculous little manifestations that money now takes its rightful place as energy and nothing more. Financial generosity lives in the modest means of the Six of Pentacles. While this card is grounded in the material and physical world, spiritual and psychic shifts are common here. Everyone longs to believe the work they do matters, and in the Six of Pentacles our heart and our work meet in the same place. We can love the challenges and setbacks as much as the victories and success because it's all ours. This is the card of the entrepreneur, the girl boss, the makers and the believers in magic every damn day.

Reinforced by: The Magician, The Chariot, Four of Wands, Nine of Cups

Opposed by: Seven of Wands, Eight of Swords, Four of Pentacles, Five of Pentacles

Seven of Pentacles—Boring Responsible Grown-Up Shit

Now that you are not whittling your bank account down to zero every pay period, you are one step closer to being a grown-up. You're a little older, a little wiser and have a little more to lose. Maybe it's time to get an accountant for your taxes rather than winging it online and hoping for the best. Phrases like managing your portfolio, savings account, investing in property and retirement planning come to mind. Needless to say, this is not the sexiest card in the deck. Delaying instant gratification for long-term rewards is a sentence that I can't even finish writing without feeling bored. It curbs the carefree spontaneity of The Fool and challenges the decadent pampering of The Empress, but it's still an important form of self-care. The abundance pipe dream of the Ace—this is how you make it happen. The cool, romantic recklessness of our youth doesn't make sense anymore, at least not all the time. But you know what else is cool? Planning a vacation a few months in advance, going out to a fancy dinner or booking a last minute plane ticket if you need to without having to check your account balance.

Reinforced by: The Emperor, Justice, Two of Pentacles, Son of Pentacles

Opposed by: The Fool, The Empress, Seven of Cups, Five of Pentacles

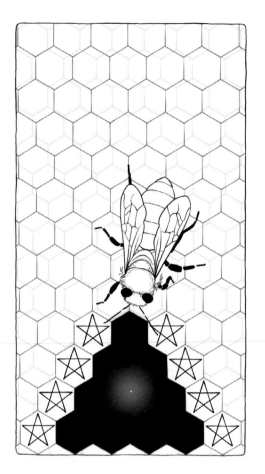

Eight of Pentacles—I Made This (and I Don't Hate It)

The epiphany of the Eight of Pentacles could occur at work, focusing on a task and realizing you actually know what the fuck you're doing. Or after work, when you hit the gym and wonder when you became a person who hits the gym. Wait, when did you start cooking healthy meals? Holy shit, your home actually smells great, and the bathroom is clean, and it's full of beautiful things. Dude, you have the best dog in the world. Wow, you really love your friends. Hey, you're so excited about that camping trip next weekend. And suddenly, you look around to find you love the life you created. Enjoy this, my love. It took years to build and it is yours. No silver spoons, no favors, no shortcuts. The Eight of Pentacles is the card of craftsmanship, of hard-work-turned-expertise, and while it can apply to a specific skill or trade, we are also the makers of our own life. In this card you discover that you've managed to build a life that is perfect, nothing is missing, you are overwhelmed by the beauty you are standing in the middle of. Damn, Gina.

Reinforced by: The Star, Judgment, Ten of Cups, Nine of Pentacles

Opposed by: The Hierophant, The Tower, Five of Swords, Seven of Cups

Nine of Pentacles—Cozy as Fuck

You worked your ass off for a long time to build this beautiful life, and in the Nine of Pentacles you are being called to let it work for you. Accomplishment, independence and nourishment are characteristic of this hard-earned card, but you no longer feel the need to flaunt it the way you once did. You are standing on the other side of charging after goals or having something to prove. The Nine of Pentacles' contentment is closely connected to a feeling of home, and celebrating this card is not a lavish affair. It is putting on your coziest pair of sweatpants and curling up by the fire on a cold winter night. People who live in the Nine of Pentacles infuse a tangible presence into the space they inhabit. When I go back to Brooklyn, I stay with my two dear friends Autumn and Chris, their rescued canary PipSqueak and Labradoodle Crackerjack. Everything in their apartment, down to the plants, is happy. Their home tells the story of a life well lived. An entire wall is lined, floor to ceiling, with books they've actually read. A large wooden hand whittled by Autumn's father sits in a corner. A worn brown leather armchair they found at a flea market rests next to an exquisite Restoration Hardware couch, finished with a coffee table they bought on the street for $25 and painted themselves. Every surface, every corner, houses trinkets accumulated from twenty years of travelling the world together. Every object feels like an heirloom and a treasure because it is theirs. I've spent hours poring through Autumn's nail polish collection, the sterling silver rings Chris used to wear, boxes of old photos and listened to the stories behind each one. Their space possesses the unique ability to fold time in on itself, and suddenly the sun is rising and the birds are chirping and a whole night was spent in laughter. It is never easy to leave. They are undeniably successful people who live in an objectively beautiful apartment, but their success translates beyond the material and the beauty of their home beyond the aesthetic. There are other, almost alchemical ingredients required to imbue a space with magic that money alone could never accomplish. No interior designer can curate that shit. It is a direct reflection of who they are.

Reinforced by: The Empress, The World, Ace of Cups, Nine of Cups, Ten of Cups
Opposed by: The Chariot, Seven of Wands, Son of Swords, Four of Cups

Ten of Pentacles—Started at the Bottom, Now We Here

You graduate college and go on a backpacking trip with two friends through Southeast Asia. Your mind is blown. You volunteer at an elephant sanctuary where you cut hundreds of pounds worth of fruit with a machete and swim in rivers with baby elephants. You ride motorbikes through the mountains. You bathe in waterfalls. You eat food that both delights and horrifies you. You never stay in a hostel that costs more then $3 a night. You travel by slow boats and sixteen-hour bus rides. You haggle with street merchants within an inch of your life. You're broke. You don't have a job lined up. You're moving to New York, one of the most expensive cities in the world, wondering how many girls you can fit into a one-bedroom apartment. A couple of decades pass. You return to Southeast Asia. Considering the flight is twenty-six hours long, you opt for first class so you can sleep on the plane. You go back to the elephant sanctuary, haggle a little less aggressively at the markets and even try your hand at motorbiking again. You fly from place to place to have more time in each city. You stay at hotels, understated in their elegance, outfitted with acclaimed restaurants and spas. As you're falling asleep one night between some deliciously soft and clean sheets, you remember a terrifying, ant-infested room you and your friends stayed in all those years ago, somewhere between Thailand and Laos, quaking with laughter as you unfolded your silk cocoon travel sheets to protect your bodies from whatever disgusting thing was certainly on the beds you would sleep in that night. It all hits you. You've amassed a level of material wealth that allows you to travel in the most comfortable, effortless way possible. The whole trip, in all of its extravagance, didn't make a dent in your bank account. Twenty-one-year-old you would bow down to present-day you. I hope you honor her. I hope you look wait staff in the eye when you order and say thank-you when they bring you your food. I hope you are kind to taxi drivers. I hope you are generous with your abundance. I hope you believe these vastly different experiences in the exact same place are equal in value.

I hope you don't forget her.

Reinforced by: The Chariot, The Devil, Seven of Pentacles, Ten of Cups

Opposed by: The High Priestess, Ace of Pentacles, Five of Pentacles, Six of Pentacles

THE
COURT CARDS

The Court Cards took me the longest to understand. In fact I'm pretty sure I gave readings for months without really knowing what they were. Pro tip: Don't do that. The difficulty with these few cards is that they most commonly represent other people. But sometimes, they can reflect an aspect of ourselves—in the past, present or future versions. When we are reading for someone, especially a stranger, we don't know all or any of the people in their life. Discerning who the fuck these people are is overwhelming and downright impossible if you are relying solely on your own intellectual prowess or powers of memorization to figure it out.

The essence of a suit is embodied in their four Court Cards, and paints a picture of what these characteristics look like in action in varying degrees of maturity and evolution. Through these cards we see what happens when pure emotionality meets mature masculinity, or the convergence of fire with the young feminine. We've already addressed the topic of gender, but it will help to remember that it does not necessarily correspond to genitals in any part of the tarot, including the Court Cards.

Knowing the traits of each Court Card and making personal connections to them helps to humanize these intimidating sixteen cards. While you make space for magic and learn to trust your intuition, you can always just ask. I've never had a client throw their arms in the air and demand a refund when I describe the qualities of the Father of Pentacles and ask if it sounds like their dad. Over time, you'll find yourself asking less.

The Court Cards are named differently depending on what deck you work with. Page, Knight, King and Queen are common, sometimes Page and Knight are swapped out for Princess and Prince, sometimes Priest and Priestess replace King and Queen, sometimes the baby is thrown out with the bathwater and we end up with The Fairy Bride, or The Master of Earth. Since we're not living in a feudal system or Candyland or my BDSM fantasy, I've found that the most immediate way to connect with the Courts is to consider them as a family unit.

Daughters—New situations, ventures or creative outlets. The naïve version of a suit's energy. Youngest of the court cards and possesses a youthful quality—either literally or being green in an aspect of life. Earth element. Connected to The Fool, the Ace cards and the Two cards.

Sons—Outward action in the world, the Sons are in a constant state of movement. Moderately experienced but still in development—in the adolescent/young adult phase—and can be brash or immature. Air element. Connected to The Chariot, the Two through Five cards.

Mothers—The characteristics of the suit internalized. Matured conception of self and others due to experience. Tied to nurturing and caring for others. Adulthood. Water element. Connected to The Empress, Strength, the Six through Nine cards.

Fathers—The long-term effects of living in a suit's energy. Can be either wise or stuck in their ways. Stabilization, success and control—they are the providers. The masculine expression of a suit in its full maturation. Fire element. Connected to The Emperor, The Hierophant, the Nine and Ten cards.

WANDS FAM
Sagittarius / Leo / Aries

It is safe to say there is never a dull moment in the Wands household—which may be a fabulous SoHo loft or an old-firehouse-turned-apartment that tastefully preserved some of the old fixtures, including the pole, on a cobblestone street in South Brooklyn. A dinner at their home may consist of impassioned arguments, loud laughter, broken glass, multiple bottles of wine, a new inspiration and last until midnight. They are fierce in all that they do. Intelligent, charismatic and hot-headed, being in their presence may feel like the fodder of reality TV. Maybe the parents have a don't-ask, don't-tell arrangement. Maybe they put the kids to bed early and have some friends over and do cocaine while the youngins sneak out through their bedroom windows to cause their own trouble. They know how to turn up and have a good time, but extreme highs and lows are both the blessing and curse of this family. The stabilizing force is the ferocity with which they love. They show us the manifestations of being ruled by fire, for better or worse.

Daughter of Wands—The Spitfire
The youngest court card of the youngest suit, the Daughter of Wands is the birth of fire. Eager to show you what she's made of and brimming with genuine enthusiasm, what she lacks in experience she will make up for with a combination of grit, intuition and stubbornness. She's a hands-on learner and quick to say yes to new adventures. Patience and prudence seem like a waste of time to this action-oriented archetype, and she will burn herself out multiple times before considering hitting the brakes. Because her energy is boundless, she is generous with it and will learn boundaries as a result of giving too much away or being taken advantage of. Crossing her is inadvisable. She will not back down from a battle and will fight dirty if she feels the situation calls for it, with betrayal topping the list of indefensible transgressions. She gives herself completely to what she loves and expects the same in return. She has a hard time comprehending that not everyone operates the way she does, but the self-centeredness is a product of youth, not narcissism.

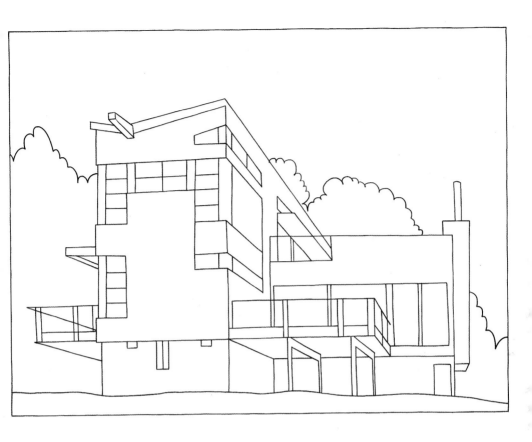

While you may see a fall coming or feel the desire to protect her from harm, don't try to tell her what to do. She will not live life on someone else's terms. She's not going to learn from your mistakes. She's going to make her own. Tons of them, in fact; but she is resilient and does not take failure personally. She is quick to fall in and out of love, quick to pick up new skills, quick to pursue new interests, quick to book plane tickets, quick to make decisions and quick to change her mind. Whether you find her whirlwind presence contagious or exhausting or both, you cannot deny that she is unapologetically herself in all that she does and puts other people at ease with her realness. She will say the outrageous thing everyone else is thinking, and while her brazen nature will not endear her to everyone, the people who love her are fierce and uncompromising in their affection. She probably has tattoos. She may horrify your parents.

Son of Wands—The Fuckboy

The appeal of the Son of Wands is undeniable. He's the hottest guy at the bar, can hold an intelligent conversation, has a great job and makes you laugh. With a knack for the grand gesture and knowing just what to say, he is easily addictive. A perfect rebound hookup, drinking buddy or friend always ready with a story about a daring adventure or some crazy girl, keep him at arms length, if you can. Maybe you laugh and roll your eyes at his stories, but you don't want to end up the subject of one. How is it that every girl he's involved with is somehow crazy? Does he find them at their prime crazy, or does he make them crazy somewhere along the way? Has he ever stopped to consider that the common denominator of all this craziness is him?

Unfortunately, this guy utilizes his considerable charms and intuition to be an asshole. Possessing a chameleon-like quality to blend into his environment, he adjusts his behavior accordingly. He is not showing you himself, he is anticipating what you want and reflecting it back to you. From the first exchange, you've been played, and it's all uphill from there. Romantic involvement with him is a death wish. He's not looking for anything serious, and being with him is trying to hold smoke. You never feel safe around him because you don't know his motivations and will likely spend hours waiting for a text back. He wears a mask so exceptionally lifelike that you don't realize it's on until you try to get closer to him and are met with walls on walls on walls. You can dig, wait, try to chip away at it, convinced there is more to find, but you won't get there. He will hurt you in order to preserve his façade. Pop culture and media only further the allure of this guy. The devil-may-care bad boy who needs a girl who challenges him, who's not like other girls, to turn him into a good guy. What is this bullshit? What's wrong with "other girls"? I like other girls. This narrative sucks.

The struggle of the Son of Wands is that he doesn't know who he is, and that is a lonely place to be. He is ruled by a fear that vulnerability, being honest about his uncertainty or allowing true intimacy, would bring rejection. His gifts are powerful but unfocused, and he needs to find an intention to concentrate his fire or risk burning the people around him, and alienating himself, with his impulses. Until he reconciles his inauthenticity and commits to his identity he is condemned to perma-fuckboy-ness.

Mother of Wands—The Real Housewife

The characteristics of this card fall somewhere between Daenerys Targaryen and Kris Jenner. In a Who Wore It Best contest, the Mother of Wands takes this round for making the suit of Wands look good. She's internalized her fire and seems to radiate with it. Her soft control over her impulses puts her in full possession of her creativity, passion and strength without tapering or suppressing them. Her role as a matriarch only emphasizes her sensual presence, and she combats the notion that one must choose between sexuality and motherhood. This is a simple concept but a revolutionary act, and the Mother of Wands is useful medicine to anyone struggling to balance their sexuality alongside other feminine expressions and responsibilities.

There are so many outlets for sexuality, with sex being only one of them. When we shut the whole thing down because we don't know how to reconcile one of its functions, we starve ourselves of essential nutrients. There is a luminous quality to the things we infuse with sexuality—it is our life-force, the basis of all creative impulse, and this is where the Mother of Wands is masterful. She walks the intuitive, nuanced line of letting this energy flow freely and in its natural form without sexualizing its recipients. This is made evident in her self-care, the generosity of her love, the beauty of her home, the freedom of her creativity, the confidence in her voice, the fluidity of her body and the intimacy within her family. The most amazing fact about the Mother of Wands to me is that she has balanced these parts of herself—heart and pelvis, love and sexuality—with perfect integrity.

She ain't perfect, though. She shares with her daughter an unwillingness to censor herself or conform to societal norms, but where the younger one is a blazing bonfire she is smoldering, inextinguishable embers. She has learned to be utilitarian with her resources. The exception to this is if you fuck with her family, then you're done. It's not personal, but she will lay you to waste. This archetype will, in a heartbeat, kill for what she loves, and under threat we see the shadow side of this powerful feminine. She will not side with the teacher when her kid gets in trouble at school and has a hard time hearing criticism of her creations. She shares a love of beauty with The Empress, and is prone to vanity, self-obsession and impulsiveness. It is not uncommon for this fiery Mother to be emotionally demanding of those around her, especially romantic partners, and she can be harsh and unforgiving if someone shows weakness or cannot keep up with her. If she has kids, she's probably a MILF.

Father of Wands—The Mogul

Everyone loves this guy. He possesses a physical presence that electrifies any room he walks into. You fight for a seat next to him at a dinner party. Under his gaze, you feel important, stimulated and giddy. The Father of Wands harnessed the latent charisma and intuition of the Son and grew it up. Here, fire meets structure, and where the Son is unfocused and destructive, the Father is a potent and dynamic energy. He's combined his creativity and his work to great effect, and he wears his success elegantly. Whether he's in jeans and a tee or a perfectly tailored suit, you know they're all made by super cool Italian designers that you've never heard of and cost more than your rent. He may be sporting a casual, understated Rolex. He is in his full power, creativity and sexuality all at once and isn't sorry about it, and no one wants him to be. You feel bigger in his presence.

Cult leader vibes, much? Kind of. When the Father of Wands appears in a reading I always wonder how much of his younger self's mask he held on to. To some degree, everyone wears a mask—whether that is necessary or not is a different matter—but his is just so fucking good. He works a room like a god. He's deeply beloved and highly regarded by friends and colleagues alike. This doesn't necessarily mean there's a catch, but there is an inevitable shadow. Too self-aware to display outright narcissism, he may harbor feelings of superiority, judgment or boredom. Close relationships with this person may result in the feeling is that he's looking at your eyes but not making eye contact. He is a big presence and will get restless if not surrounded by people he considers equals. What's most disconcerting about this man is that he knows he is capable of using his powers in light and dark, and has done both over the course of his lifetime. His sensitivity and ability to read people makes him capable of great compassion, and also masterful manipulation. Matthew McConaughey is a Father of Wands, but so is Charles Manson. At worst, he's appeared in readings as a perpetrator.

The impact of the Father of Wands is a powerful one, but in what capacity can be unclear. To remain in the light, he must hold himself to high standards of integrity, surround himself with people who match him and find healthy outlets for excess energy.

SWORDS FAM
Gemini / Libra / Aquarius

When you seek out the Swords Family house, you end up in the suburbs, in a neighborhood chosen for its low crime rate and excellent public school system. Dinner consists of a protein, vegetable and starch and is on the table at 6:30 p.m. every night. It's pretty good. It would be better with wine, but there is none in the house. The conversation is perfunctory and polite, consisting of summarizing their days and goings-on at school or work. No voices are raised. Dinner ends at 7:15, by which time you're really, really fucking bored. Routine and structure are the backbones of this family makeup, and the environment can feel severe, dry and strict. They are financially stable but never showy with it, preferring to smartly invest. This family gets a bad rap because they're a drag and zero fun, but their stability is unwavering and their integrity second to none. Their kids will always be safe, always have dependable parents and always be loved—perhaps expressed through actions and deeds and not words. Talking about feelings is not the strong suit of the Swords. They are highly intelligent and feel more comfortable in the realms of rationality and logic than tenderness and intuition. Though the intentions are good, living in this atmosphere is both creatively and emotionally stifling. They probably don't believe in magic.

Daughter of Swords—The Killjoy
She doesn't mean to, but the Daughter of Swords is the well-meaning ruiner of everything. A chronic overthinker, she will suck the life out of a possibility before it even happens by mapping out every possible negative outcome. The curse of this Daughter is that she cannot be fully present in any situation. She is always watching herself from above in a state of self-censorship. She is a perfectionist and can be critical of others, but rarely to the extent she is with herself, and is crippled as a result. Obsessive, nervous and prone to anxiety, she probably bites her nails. Spontaneity is impossible for this cautious archetype, and it can be painful to watch the ways she refuses to be an active participant in her own life. It can also illuminate where we are too harsh with ourselves, or where we hold ourselves back out of self-consciousness. She is the voice in our head that cuts excitement and dilutes optimism. Whether it is to save from potential disappointment or to remain controlled in the moment, the effect is the same. Due to fear, we did not allow ourselves to fully experience something.

If you are able to coax the Daughter of Swords out of her shell, you will most likely find someone very sweet, a little callow and smart as hell. Her powers of observation are uncanny, and her advice is fair and balanced. You trust her as an objective source on emotional matters, and her energy is an antidote to hysteria or weepiness. Her practicality is especially appreciated when we are feeling helpless, and she can see a possible course of action that we may have missed. She is a loyal friend, always honest, never reckless and will save you from disaster over the course of your relationship. Occasionally, she may even let you copy her math homework.

Son of Swords—The Agro

This card brings to mind a dude like Steve Jobs or Ari Gold. Great, accomplished men. Geniuses with absolutely no chill. Being around someone in this energy is hard on the nervous system because he is in a state of constant movement, ever charging ahead at full speed. Intensity is not a negative characteristic, but the type displayed by the Son of Swords can feel a little bloodless. It does not translate to the tireless efforts of a passionate individual, but rather the militant force of a soldier. This could be due to the fact that his brilliance is more technical than artistic, but either way he's not what you'd call a people person. He's scary and intimidating and makes others uncomfortable. He might be the friend you feel like you have to invite to a party but secretly hope he doesn't come.

Being well-liked is of little consequence to the Son of Swords; he is singular in his focus and urgent in his mission. His bravery can be seen in the way he pushes boundaries, of his own endurance and of the field he works in. The demands he places on himself are extreme. His standards are in a category of their own. He is not interested in perfection, because that is a pre-existing paradigm. He wants to go beyond what has been done before. He shares the quality of obsessive thinking with the Daughter of Swords, but where she internalizes it, he represents its outward manifestation. His insane expectations make him a difficult, if not impossible, person to work with—with colleagues often feeling freaked out, diminished or alienated. Team player is not on his list of special skills. But he also made Apple.

The mystery of the Son of Swords is what motivates him? A love of discovery? A desire to prove himself? Unemotional and indifferent to the opinions of others, it seems unlikely. Maybe he is driven by a need to make a contribution, or to know what he is capable of. Addiction cannot be ruled out, either. Often, the advice of this card is to seriously consider if a situation calls for such an aggressive and excessive approach.

In a romantic capacity, one must wonder what it might feel like to be the focus of his gaze. Personally, I'd swipe left. He's the stuff of clingers and stalkers and gives off some serious SVU realness. A balanced relationship will not occur here, and he tends to attract partners who are either insecure and enjoy being worshipped or are heavily guarded because he has no problem ignoring boundaries. If you're waiting for someone to come and break down your walls, it's this guy. Careful what you wish for.

The challenge of the Son of Swords is to better know himself and his motivations. His energy stabilizes if he can infuse his intense nature with passion and purpose, and diffuse it altogether when the situation calls for it.

Mother of Swords—That Bitch You Don't Wanna Fuck With

The Mother of Swords has been burned in the past—badly, perhaps repeatedly—and is not going to let that happen again. She shut down her heart for the sake of protecting it, and she had her reasons, but she never went back to retrieve it. She's got trust issues she never sought therapy for. She craves connection but cannot ask for it and refuses it when it comes her way. As a result, attempts at vulnerability come off stunted, translating as victimhood and blaming. You're never comfortable around her. Her passive aggression borders on aggression at all times, and anything you say could make her snap at you.

Honestly, she's a bitch. She is sharp, jaded, mistrustful and quick to assume the worst about others. She rarely forgives and never forgets. Hurt people hurt people, and her cruelty is extra, utilizing her intelligence, pain and whatever she knows about you to go in for the kill. She confuses coldness for strength. She may feel a sense of pride for her paranoia, citing it as discernment. She justifies her behaviors because of what she's been through and is motivated by self-preservation.

This is no way to go through life. Healing is needed here. Maybe you want her as your divorce attorney, maybe you want to team up with her when you need to put your bad-bitch face on and play hardball with life, or negotiate with someone who isn't taking you seriously or fight in at war, but beyond that she is severely limited. A strict mother, a frigid partner and a volatile boss, try to avoid entering into relationships with people like this involving power dynamics where they have authority over you.

When the Mother of Swords shows up in a reading, we are asked to examine the fortress built around our hearts. How thick are the walls, how strong are the reinforcements, why did we take these protective measures in the first place and do we need them anymore? If not, thank the Mother of Swords for her service and release her. You may find a wounded inner child in need of care. You may find a heart that is intact and stronger than you previously thought.

Father of Swords—The Dad Who Always Knows Where Your Paperwork Is

This dad has his shit together, and he has your shit together too. Where I throw away important documents (without shredding them) because I don't know where to put them and they're probably online, anyway, the Father of Swords has a home office with file cabinets full of those things you never think about until you need them. Your tax return from 2004? No problem. Your medical records for the last fifteen years? He'll fax them right over. Organization is how he makes sense of the world around him. He's integrated the intellect and technical mastery of his Son and is well suited for jobs like accountant, lawyer, scientist or analyst. The people he works with know him to be fair, hardworking and pragmatic. He is an excellent leader and fair boss. His integrity is on point.

The Father of Swords always makes me a little sad because he is an amazing dad who would do anything for his kids, but his mental intelligence far surpasses his emotional intelligence, and he is therefore largely mysterious to himself. He won't write you a long, heartfelt birthday card, but he will keep you on his health insurance until you're twenty-six, pay your phone bill and help you get a new social security card when you lose yours. He expresses his love by showing up, and that's not bad. It's better than the Fuckboy who will wax poetic about his love for you and then ghost. It's difficult to tell if the Father of Swords is happy. I don't think he even knows.

Truly emotionally connecting with this person is challenging, kind of awkward, and they will never initiate it. With a father figure especially, it may be difficult to discover that, while he's such a boss in other areas of his life, he is very young emotionally.

CUPS FAM
Cancer / Scorpio / Pisces

You catch a train upstate to Woodstock to check out the Cups Family house. It's an old barn with high ceilings and big plant-lined windows. The walls are covered in art. You look around and see records, the Son taking paintbrush to canvas, braids of garlic hanging from the ceiling and an eclectic and charmingly mismatched collection of furniture. The Daughter greets you, wearing a rainbow tutu and glitter eye shadow, hands you a flower and reads your palm. The Mother calls hello from the kitchen, pots and pans on all burners, and whatever she's cooking smells like home. They're hippies. Are you on a commune? You feel at ease. It's a nice night, so you eat outside at a weathered picnic table, heavily carved with drawings, messages and initials. Fresh flowers adorn the table and candles flicker in their votives. You drink mead. The meal is an old family recipe, complete with vegetables from their garden, and you've never eaten anything so delicious. You ask for seconds and have to refuse thirds. You ask where the Father is, and the Mother laughs and brings out some moonshine. You don't bring him up again. You crash on the couch because you're too drunk to get home, and you don't feel awkward about it. The next morning, the Mother sends you off with a tupperware full of leftovers.

Daughter of Cups—The Space Cadet

The dreamers, violet children and Luna Lovegoods of the world align with the energy of the Daughter of Cups. The world hasn't beaten the shit out of her yet and—though her spaciness can be frustrating and unreliable—you hope it never will. If she's an older person, she has somehow managed to protect her sense of wonder from the elements, to lovely results. She pursues what she finds to be beautiful and interesting with no real end—a novelty in this goal-oriented and career-motivated world. If you can hold her attention long enough, she will delight you with her proficiency in poetry and literature. She learned massage therapy in Costa Rica and did a yoga teacher training in India. She is fluent in three languages. Her art floors you, and you don't even know anything about art. When you ask if she's ever thought about selling it, she shrugs off the question. When you tell her you know a gallery owner you could connect her with, she changes the subject.

Relationships with the Daughter of Cups can be baffling because they are sitting atop a goldmine of unharvested talent. It's especially annoying when they're a starving artist and can't pay their rent. The Daughter of Cups isn't very good at being a human. The logistics of life do not hold her interest, and she probably hasn't done her taxes in three years.

Be gentle with her and with this part of yourself. She is the source of all creative inspiration. The muse. She embodies the purest experience of awe, wonder and reverence humans are capable of. It is easy to ignore this, and she will not fight for your attention. Almost everything is more pressing and time-sensitive than what she offers us, but few things are as nourishing.

Son of Cups—The Art Bro

This sellout decided that it wasn't realistic to make a living selling his paintings, so compromised by getting a job in advertising that has the word art in its title. He's a hippie turned hipster who traded in the commune for thick-framed glasses and skinny jeans, but he still wears his dad's old flannels. Honestly, he's not a sellout, he probably wasn't going to make a living selling his paintings, and there was nothing going on upstate anyway. In the Son of Cups, we see a harmonious reconciliation of femininity by a masculine energy. So let's give him a break, okay? While a starving artist is a frustrating cliché, nothing seems to boil people's blood more than a profitable one.

The Son of Cups applied form and function to the Daughter's creativity in order for it to evolve alongside him, the act of which includes inevitable compromise. Even people living the artistic dream must negotiate the world around them. Artists have to price their work, coordinate with gallery owners, acquiesce to loyal patrons and make a website. Musicians must be in agreement with their bandmates, travel, consider the tastes of their audience, manage their social media and book and pay for time in a recording studio. And with all of it, there is the issue of profit as a contaminant. Grounding fluid creative energy into the structure of the physical world is an ongoing challenge, and the Son of Cups navigates it with grace and success. He's supporting himself off his work. That's hot.

Now that you mention it, he's kind of hot, isn't he? He's got that understated, boy-next-door thing going for him, and his appeal only grows when you get to know him. He's mysterious but also knowable, a hopeless romantic with a rich emotional landscape. When imbalanced, he can be depressive, moody and retreat into fantasy. He's probably a generous lover.

Mother of Cups—The (Slightly Co-Dependent) Nurturer

The Mother of Cups is going to scoop you into a hug the second you meet her, and not one of those limp, one-armed travesties. She genuinely wants to embrace you, and you want to let her. Her warmth immediately puts people at ease, and you may find yourself pouring your heart out to her. She is openhearted and inclusive, qualities that inspire vulnerability in everyone she meets. Being guarded doesn't make sense, or feel necessary, in her presence. She's an old soul. Both psychic and empathetic, she awakens our desire to be seen and accepted and offers herself up for the job. Cut out to be a therapist, social worker or nurse, she is naturally inclined toward helping others. She will intuitively connect with any healing modality she pursues, spiritual or otherwise. If she decides to offer it professionally, it won't look much different than what she's been doing her entire life. She is a born healer through and through.

The shadow of the Mother of Cups is that she doesn't know who she is if she's not taking care of other people. Her identity is informed by her ability to nurture others, and setting boundaries will be more difficult for her than any of the other Court Cards. She is most comfortable putting the spotlight on others and can be reluctant to talk about herself. While she is a big energy, she is self-conscious about occupying too much space. She will give you the shirt off her back, but is that a good thing? She's passing out on the airplane because she put on other people's air masks before her own.

The inevitable eventuality the Mother of Cups lives with is that she will have to reckon with this co-dependence at some point, but rarely will it be a product of people convincing her to do so. It could be that her kids leave the nest, or she otherwise finds herself alone. A crisis or spiritual awakening could also lead her to seek fulfillment internally.

Father of Cups—The Broken Man

Worst dad award goes to this guy. The Father of Cups appears in readings in varying degrees of absence. He could be an alcoholic or addict, or suffer from mental illness or chronic depression. Maybe he physically abandoned his family. Maybe he never resolved shit with his dad and is rife with unhealed trauma. Or he could just be emotionally checked out. The result is the same: He is unreachable.

The tragedy of the Father of Cups is that he possesses great depth and an unlimited creative potential, but he never explored either. Maybe he couldn't or wouldn't. It's possible that financial security, prestige, notions of masculinity or external expectations informed his decision to ignore his watery nature, but here we see the tax collected from neglecting your essence. The creativity rotted into destruction, and he is drowning in his own depths. The Father of Cups depicts emotionality collapsed in on itself.

It is possible that, outwardly, the Father of Cups seems very successful. He abandoned what he wanted and needed and was called to do in favor of what he thought he should do, and it's likely he's good at it. He is respected for his diplomacy, generosity and ability to manage a positive working environment. He may even show hints of a former, abandoned self at times, but it's a drop of water on a sun-scorched landscape.

If I'm reading for the Father of Cups, the message is to rediscover yourself. You may have to dismantle a lot of long-standing structures in order to do so, but whatever mess may be made in this process carries less consequence than staying the course. If I'm reading for someone who has the Father of Cups in their life, the urging is to walk away. The shadow of this person is quicksand. They probably won't change, and in the ways that matter, they are already gone.

PENTACLES FAM
Taurus / Virgo / Capricorn

You approach the sprawling Westchester mansion of the Pentacles Family, and it's huge and tasteful at the same time. Ivy crawls up the stone walls and the landscaping is the kind of perfect that takes a team of people. You pull out your phone and look up the address to find you're staring at a nine million dollar house. You decide you hate these people before you walk in the door. The Mother greets you and you're surprised you weren't let in by the help. She takes your coat and offers you a scotch. You love scotch. Fuck, that's good scotch. You wonder if you're underdressed. You feel like you should've taken your shoes off, but everyone else is wearing theirs. You wonder how the floors are so clean. Dinner is served in the formal dining room, and goddamnit it's delicious. The Mother apologizes for the lack of meat and explains that she's a vegetarian for ethical reasons and since she's the one cooking, everyone else has to deal with it. You register that there is no maid and no personal chef. You're also a vegetarian, also for ethical reasons, and you kind of love her for a second. The children are charming and mild-mannered, if not a little serious. The Son is an engineer, and the Daughter just found out she is Ivy-bound. The Father is older, distinguished and kind. They are curious about you. They ask engaging questions and, aside from occasional mentions of Montana mountain houses and summering in the Hamptons, you feel comfortable and connected to them. At the end of the meal, to toast the Daughter's college acceptance, the Father disappears into the wine cellar and comes back with a very old and very expensive looking bottle of champagne, the delicacy of which is lost on you. Dinner lasts longer than you thought it would. You like everyone. The secret pill addiction, undertones of despair, miserable looking hired-help or kids playing nice to stay in the will that you were expecting to find—it's just not there. They're actually happy. On the way home, you call your therapist.

Daughter of Pentacles—The Nice Girl

The Daughter of Pentacles did everything right. From the AP classes and extracurriculars to the SAT prep and community service, she checks off the boxes of a well-rounded candidate. An adolescence-worth of diligence put her in a good position. Her resume is a masterpiece. When we meet the Daughter of Pentacles, she is contemplating her next move, and girl's got options.

On paper she is perfect, and in her short life she has made a lot of mature decisions, but she is not an adult. Upon meeting, you may find her weighing the pros and cons of five different Ivy League schools, but if you ask what she's majoring in you'll find she's undecided. She's certainly better off for the success she set herself up for, but she doesn't yet have the faculties to fully appreciate that. A little Pollyanna, a little doe-eyed, a little more style than substance, the Daughter of Pentacles stands on the solid ground of a sheltered childhood, gazing out at a successful adolescence.

Growing up will add street smarts to her considerable book smarts, but as it stands now she's basic. She wears Uggs. She loves pizza. Her comforter is pink. Sometimes she breaks curfew, but for the most part she's not making any waves. If asked to describe her, you would say she is a very nice girl. There is a distinct lack of character in the Daughter of Pentacles due to her naivety and youth. She's not going to spice up your life, but your mom will love her.

This is the picture of many kids going off to college, sometimes investing or borrowing hundreds of thousands of dollars to study a subject their undeveloped, teenage brains decided they want to pursue for the rest of their life. College institutions normalize this insanity, long-woven into the fabric of the American Dream. But if it wasn't, under what other circumstances would we give a teenager that much money and let them make a decision this big?

First and foremost, the Daughter of Pentacles is a student. She is open-minded and willing to consider new experiences. When she shows up in a reading it is an indication that there is a lesson available. Keep your eyes open for it. More literally, you may be called to go back to school or seek additional training, bring in a mentor or otherwise get learned.

Son of Pentacles—The Nerd

The Son of Pentacles and Son of Swords have much in common, and often they will show up alongside each other in a reading as different aspects of, or options for, the same person. The most notable difference is the pacing—where the Son of Swords is giving you anxiety because of his no chill, the Son of Pentacles is slow and steady. What he lacks in natural brilliance he makes up for in industriousness. He's not going to push boundaries or take wild risks, and he's probably not going to invent the next Internet. He will, however, accomplish his goal. A more sustainable energy than his Swords counterpart, he understands that some efforts just take time.

If the Daughter of Pentacles was waiting on or deciding between opportunities, then the Son of Pentacles got it and is grinding away. His professional aspirations are the backbone of his identity, the throughline through which all other priorities are set. He will work weekends and holidays if necessary. He doesn't fly out of the office as soon as his shift is up. He's not going to have another drink because he has work the next morning. He's the responsible friend who makes you question your poor life choices.

There is an unglamorous reality that lives between the conception of a dream and its manifestation, and most of that reality is the Son of Pentacles. He gets flack for being a stubborn, socially-awkward square, but he's the one laughing all the way to the bank. Exceedingly diligent, dedicated and focused, there is nothing he cannot accomplish. Sometimes there is boring work required to harness a vision and root it into the ground. But it's more boring to have a bunch of pipe dreams, unlaid plans and great ideas that die on the vine.

Mother of Pentacles—The Earth Goddess

You can find the Mother of Pentacles in the woods, communing with nature. She may be gathering herbs for a tincture, feeding the chickens or tending to her garden. A materially abundant but not materialistic person, her connection to the physical can be found in her strong relationship with nature, animals and other people.

She is a force who feels at home on the earth and in her body. She offers no apologies for her enjoyment of the finer things in life, sensual pleasures or prosperity. Staying grounded comes naturally to her, and her physical abundance is matched by her generosity and service. Well suited for the professions of teacher, herbalist, wildlife rehabilitator, farmer or maker, she will thrive in all areas that call for physical connection and elemental understanding. She is a born green witch.

Even if she's married to a sugar daddy, she has a job or is otherwise self-supporting. Self-possession and independence are big motivators for the Mother of Pentacles, and she will preserve her sense of personal security and identity no matter the circumstance.

Motherhood and homesteading are second nature to this earth energy, and she derives fulfillment from tending to the world around her. The work of this extrovert will be finding out where she ends and others begin. Overwatering and drought are equally lethal, and there is a time where the thing you birthed no longer requires your care. Your children will leave home. The wild animal you rehabilitated will return to the woods. The vegetables you planted will be called to harvest. And you will still be there. It's bittersweet and ripe for discovery.

Father of Pentacles—The Sugar Daddy

The card of CEOs, sugar daddies and presidents, wealth is the defining characteristic of the Father of Pentacles. And not only is he rich, but he's been rich for long enough that he no longer freaks out about the fact that he's rich. He's chilling. He doesn't walk into his handsome study and marvel at the rows of leather-bound first editions. He doesn't pour himself a scotch from the crystal decanter on the marble table and giggle because he's not drinking cheap whiskey out of the bottle. He's settled comfortably into his abundant reality. An older masculine, he is probably past the height of his career and enjoying the fruits born from a lifetime of hard work. His distinction, authority and prosperity are a given. He wears it loosely and with ease.

For the Father of Pentacles, to love is to provide for, and a father figure like him means you will never go without. If you can't make rent that month, if you really want to take that vacation, if you decide to go back to school, you are covered. Under certain circumstances, he may draft a document detailing the interest-free loan and proposed payment plan. That is for your sake, not his. His satisfaction with his life comes from the work he put into creating it, with money being only one of the many by-products. It is important that the people he loves both feel supported and appreciate the value of an honest day's work.

Because of his strong connection to the material world, the Father of Pentacles will falter if his physical resources are compromised. Ill health, financial hardship or family problems will all threaten the foundation of this sturdy masculine. In cases like these, he risks collapse if he does not reach for the immaterial. Emotional support and spiritual connection open doors for further development and expansion.

WHAT THE FUCK ARE TAROT SPREADS?

A spread is the physical formation in which you lay out the cards. Each position indicates a different factor and further informs the meaning of the cards. There are more tarot spreads than there are tarot decks, ranging from general life spreads to excruciatingly specific. I do not use a different spread depending on the topic, mostly because I'm too dumb to memorize a thousand different spreads. And also because the cards will speak for themselves. There is no need to overly tailor a spread to match a question.

Do not be rigid about tarot spreads, if you feel like a card wants to say more, or you want to dive deeper into a certain aspect, pull another card. I use spreads as a way of initiating a conversation with the tarot, but the conversation continues over the course of a reading. Sometimes a reading ends with all seventy-eight cards on the table. Sometimes, the initial spread speaks for itself. Usually, it is somewhere in the middle.

How you lay out the cards is a matter of preference. Some people pull cards for a spread one at a time, or pull the cards face-down and reveal them one at a time. In my experience, how a spread all connects together informs the reading from the very beginning, so I pull them all at once and let them speak as a unit as well as individually. I know readers who will do multiple spreads over the course of one reading, discarding the cards covering a topic once it is finished. Either they will put them back in the deck and shuffle again to address another matter, or just pull from the remaining cards in the deck. My approach is a holistic one, keeping all cards on the table and letting them layer on top of each other as the reading progresses. Experiment with different ways of laying out the cards during a reading and see what feels most natural to you.

When you introduce a spread, pay attention to what the cards look like together, who is facing what, etc. Is a card looking off into nothing? Pull another card. If a dark card appears, I will pull additional cards to dig to the root of the issue. So much of tarot is connecting with your intuition, and this is a place where a formula is constricting rather than useful. With that said, there are some spreads that I have found to be effective jumping-off points when starting a reading.

Everything Spread

This is my most used and trusted spread. In a general reading, the spread invites in several aspects of life and identifies where they most impact a person's life. If inquiring about something specific, it illustrates the layers and effects of that particular situation. Mind, body and spirit can be seen as the ego, superego and id, or the conscious, subconscious and unconscious. In these cards, we are digging through layers of awareness. Mind is the forefront of our consciousness, whereas body and then spirit increase in vulnerability and depth. Past, present and future are the external circumstances of life, what the person is manifesting as a result of their internal environment. The external and internal snapshot of this spread provides a holistic view of a situation. When I use this spread, I view each of the six cards as a doorway through which more can be revealed by dialogue with the querist and additional cards.

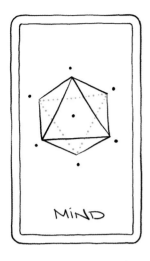 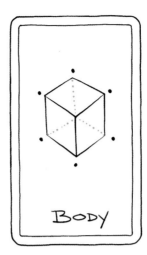 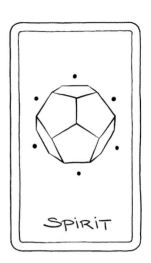

MiND BODY SPiRiT

PAST PRESENT FUTURE

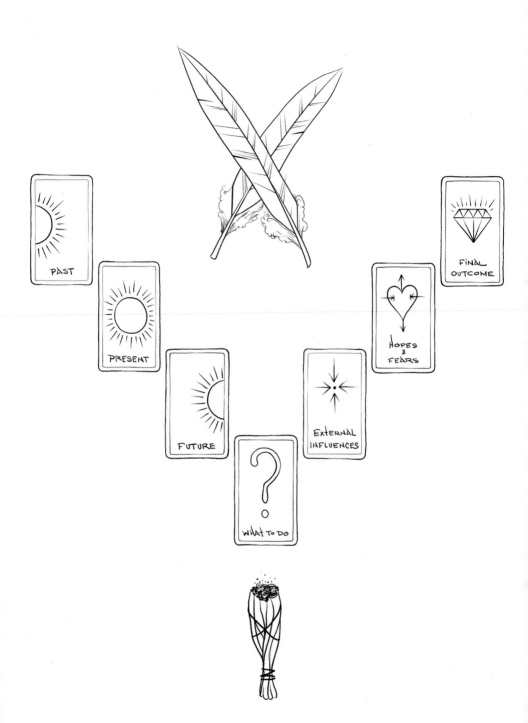

PAST

PRESENT

FUTURE

WHAT TO DO

EXTERNAL INFLUENCES

HOPES & FEARS

FINAL OUTCOME

Ellipse Spread

This "quick and dirty" spread is one I use when doing a reading on one specific question or situation. That thing or person that we cannot stop thinking about no matter what we do? This spread is good for that. It allows for complete immersion into the situation, examines it from every angle and also provides specific instruction on what to do and the likely outcome from the recommended action.

Chakra Spread

Chakras are seven energy centers in the body that correspond to different physical, emotional and spiritual functions. Beginning at the base of the spine and going up to the top of the head, it is believed that this is the direction in which energy flows into and through our bodies. When something occurs that disrupts or blocks this circulation it can lead to maladies of all sorts. The Chakra spread is useful if you or the person you are reading for has a question about their body, or is feeling the physical impact of a mental or spiritual block. Chakras can be either overcharged or undercharged, and either will result in imbalance. A good spread to use preceding Reiki or bodywork, as it gives a map of where attention is most needed. Read more about Chakras on pages 139 to 141.

HOW THE FUCK DO I GIVE A READING?

Regardless of how much preparation you do, the best way to get to know your cards is to use them. It is impossible to build confidence in yourself as a reader without doing this. I will repeat: You're not gonna learn to read for people without reading for people. Interact with your cards in this way as soon as possible. Being over-prepared can lead to over-thinking and make it all the more terrifying. Luckily, when you tell people you read tarot, specifically for free when you're just starting out, you will be bombarded with opportunities to practice.

I gave a reading to a girlfriend the first day I received my deck. Yes, I stumbled over their meanings, consulted the guidebook and said uhh a lot—but the message of the cards was clear regardless. She just got out of a relationship, and it was the kind of breakup that wrecks your shit. The can't-get-out-of-bed, don't-want-to-eat, wake-up-to-pure-misery, life-is-meaningless kind of breakup. The cards showed another romantic interest entering her life shortly thereafter, an unfathomable concept when you're in the depths of breakup hell. It suggested she let the breakup be clean—no late night texting, no trying to get back together shenanigans—so she could be as healed as possible for this next person soon entering her life.

Two months later, she met the man who is now her husband.

Let the cards show you they work. This experience was not a one-off, or beginner's luck. This shit works, as crazy (see: magic) as it is. Building confidence in this area is not unlike building muscle—you have to repeatedly exercise your intuition in order to strengthen it. For the first year of giving readings I was waiting for the one that I would fuck up and get totally wrong. It never came. There was no other way to alleviate that fear than stepping into it over and over again.

There are certain milestones I can pinpoint that helped solidify my confidence. Times when something incredibly specific came to mind—so specific that, if it were off, it would have totally killed the vibe—and I said it. The first time I delivered information in a reading that I knew my client didn't want to hear. When I intuited an image that made no sense to me but made perfect sense to the person. Simply, my confidence built each time I decided to believe my impressions. When I stopped worrying about being wrong.

These moments all exemplify why tarot is more than mere memorization. Ego will get in the way of intuition every single time. Dismantling the ego and learning to trust your intuition is one of the hardest things I've ever done. Opening my heart to my clients and learning to sit with them in their vulnerability and need is one of the hardest things I've ever done. These are not optional components of reading for others—they are base requirements. If you do not possess the willingness to let yourself open in this way, you have no business being a healer. I know this sounds harsh, but hear me out.

When I first started reading I was high on my ego. Here's this super magical cool thing I can do. About a month into it, a man came to me for a reading. His wife just died, and he wanted to know how he was supposed to keep living without her. About a week later, a girl around my age came to me and told me she knew she was sexually assaulted as a child but needed help recovering the memory. This is not a party trick. These are real people coming to you with real need and depending on you as a guide. It is a sacred responsibility, and if there is any one piece of guidance you take away from this book, it is to treat that responsibility with care and humility or do not take it on at all.

With that said, it is better to approach a reading feeling like you don't know anything than thinking you have it all figured out. After years of reading professionally, the cards still surprise, teach and humble me each time I use them. To think we have the cards on lock is to think that we already possess an understanding of any possible individual person and their experience. The meanings of the cards will be as varied as the people you read for.

How the fuck do you give a reading? You just pick a spread and a person and do the damn thing, boo. The cards will take it from there if you let them.

Tarot Reading FAQ for Noobs

When giving a reading, what do I do first?

Take some time with the person before jumping in to pull cards for them. Depending on where you are, have your setup ready—the bare minimum of which is two seats with a surface in between to lay the cards out. Think about the best way to make you and the client feel comfortable, whether it is engaging in some chit chat or starting off with a quiet moment. I tend to ask my clients a few innocuous questions at the beginning—where they're coming from, inquiring about something they're wearing, how about this fucking weather, huh?—before jumping into the realness. For returning clients, its nice to briefly touch base, and for new clients, it aids in snapping them out of any anxiety or awkwardness they may feel coming into a reading.

Do you talk to a client at length before a reading starts? If so, about what?

This is something that you, as the reader, can decide upon beforehand or leave up to your client. I have some people come in and they won't say a word before we start either because they're skeptical and want to test me or are otherwise unwilling to give details about what's going on. After the aforementioned small talk is over (run time of which is approximately two minutes), I ask if there is anything they want their reading to be focused on or based around, any area or aspect of their life where they feel like they need more clarity, or direction. When people come uncertain of what to focus on, I advise them to ask about the matter that is sitting heaviest in their heart. I also let them know a reading can be left completely open, and we can begin with a general overview. It is worth noting that a general reading becomes specific very quickly, but that we let the cards decide what to focus on rather than setting the intention beforehand. This is the case one in every five times, with people typically coming for readings aware of what their intention is going into it, and willing to share that with you. I used to be scared of the people who didn't say anything before a reading started, but I have come to prefer that over clients who spend the first twenty minutes of their reading explaining their circumstances in-depth. This is not a therapy session, and getting bogged down in the details of a story is not necessary for you as the reader or helpful for them as the client. If they do want to share information, I try to limit it to five minutes of conversation before drawing cards. I have found this is a healthy balance of starting a reading at an appropriate level of depth—you don't have to do the time-wasting guess-work of "it seems like this is a love reading" but you also don't have too much subjective narrative cluttering your ability to cut to the heart of the matter.

How do I start pulling cards?

After speaking to your client and solidifying the intention, shuffle the cards however you like. I tend to start shuffling the moment I sit down with them, during the chit-chat, and keep going until we're ready to start the reading. Depending on how the conversation goes, this is the point where I decide what spread I will use for their reading. I give them the deck to cut, however they like, and however many times they like, and then put it back together. I am not particular about this. Some readers have their clients cut the deck three times in a certain direction with their left hand. Sure, why not? Regardless, the deck will not be put back together wrong. When they hand it back to you, take a breath, focus your intention, say a prayer and pull the damn things.

How will I know when to pull more cards?

Any time you feel like you're about to say uhh or feel a desire to dig deeper into a card's meaning, pull another card. Any time it seems like there is something more to a story, pull another card. If something doesn't feel right, pull another card. Don't be precious about this.

How will I know when I am done with the reading?

In a perfect world, every reading ends the same way as good sex—decisively, intuitively and with both parties feeling satisfied. While my readings have a run time of one hour, I never set a timer for them. Maybe it's magic, maybe it's practice, maybe I've given enough readings to get into a groove of arcing a reading around the length of an hour, but they just seem to naturally end right at the hour mark. For me, a reading ending feels like a door closing, a definitive feeling that all information available to that person to aid them in their intention has been delivered. I leave a small window of time at the end to ask them if they have any questions, but this is to follow up on what's already been covered. In less than ideal scenarios, clients will push for more time or open up a completely new topic at the end of a reading. If it can be answered in a couple of cards, I will let it happen. But, if at the fifty-seven minute mark someone says "but what about my family?" I let them know this is a subject too complicated to be appropriately assessed in the remaining time. It's not the best feeling in the world, but the client doesn't always have to be happy in order for a reading to be complete. I've painted comprehensive, practical pictures for clients of how to move forward from where they are, and sometimes where they are is such a shitshow that it doesn't look a whole lot better than where they are at the current time. This is okay. You are not a performing monkey. You are not reading tarot to tell people what they want to hear. If you feel like you do not have more information for them, that is how you know the reading is over.

I know you mention that it's hard to be wrong if you are aligned with your intuition, but real talk, what do you do when the person you're reading for says you're wrong?

Alright my sweet, scared, doe-eyed little peaches. The honest-to-god truth is I don't really know how to answer this question. I waited for this nightmarish moment for years before accepting it probably wouldn't happen. Granted, I don't go into the depth that some mediums and intuitives do. I'm not going to try to pull your grandmother's name out of thin air or intuit the city your father is from. If this type of energy reading is something you are interested in, this book is not a resource for that and here's why: When giving a reading, I channel information from the highest available energetic source, which actually is not the person I'm reading for. It's their higher self; the spirit-clique, angel squad that reflects a truth greater and truer than a person's immediate perception of it. Specific information and details come in at a denser vibration as they are, really, of no consequence to the message and heart of the matter. However, they can be important if someone is coming in skeptical. Mediums—people who channel the departed—pull information from this more human, slightly heavier energetic layer to offer their clients "proof of the living mind," of the person coming through. It can be as specific as a name or a relationship or as vague as a smell, but it will always be something that allows the client to recognize the person trying to communicate with them. I don't like doing mediumship. I find it viscerally invasive and emotionally draining. I will allow it in if it comes through during a reading, but I do not ask for it. I'm saying all this because these are the cold, hard facts that you can be objectively wrong about. I would advise not trying to provide information like this unless it specifically presents itself to your through your intuition. If you're wrong, that's okay. Ask a clarifying question and move on.

What I have experienced is abrasive, obnoxious clients who come in not wanting to hear the truth. One of them came into my apartment with a dog she didn't ask to bring with her, refused to take her shoes off when I requested she do so and then sighed and rolled her eyes for the first fifteen minutes of her reading. When I asked her what the issue was, she let me know that absolutely everything I said was wrong and nothing I said made sense to her. The cards were illuminating that her combative nature was preventing her from seeing professional success and personal intimacy. I refunded her and asked her to leave. A reader I love and trust once sent a person home within moments of meeting them because she said she was unable to intuitively plug into that person's energetic field.

The best advice I can give you on being wrong in a reading does not differ much from being wrong in life—when you are, correct it and move on. When you're not, trust your integrity, hold your ground and do not let yourself be bulldozed by assholes.

Daily Draw

I no longer read for myself. I've found that while I can be an impartial mirror to my clients, I am too personally invested in myself and what happens to me to act as a clear channel. If I pull the Death card for a client, I can discern whether it signifies the ending of an idea or a phase of life or a relationship. When I pull Death for myself I'm quite certain I will die in the next five minutes. We have ways we want situations in our life to turn out, and I find myself imposing my will, or my fear, over the true meaning of the cards.

However, while I was still familiarizing myself with the tarot I pulled one card for myself every morning. In addition to lending an intentional framework to your day, this is an effective method of cultivating a personal relationship with your deck. I noticed certain cards appeared repeatedly, or that people in my life continually showed up as the same card. There is no way to separate your readings from your personal connections to the cards, nor should you try. If a card shows itself to you over and over again as the fuckboy card, if you come to associate one of the images with travel, if a traditionally positive card comes up as a warning, just go with it. This dedicated practice will, over time, cultivate an intimacy with the cards in a way little else will. At the end of the day, revisit the card you pulled and see how your day connected to the meaning of that card. You'll find yourself saying, "Damn, this was such a Hanged Man day" or "Wow, that work meeting today was so Three of Wands I can't even." So maybe you don't talk like me (and good for you), but the point is these personal associations help create context when reading for others.

The Shitty Cards

One of the main reasons the tarot is such an accurate divinatory tool is because of the balance of light and dark in the cards. There are Angel and Oracle decks that are pretty much all Love & Light, Wonder, Healing and the like. Vomit. That is not the tarot, nor is it a way to get an honest depiction of someone's circumstances. We all have darkness. We may suppress it or hide it or not know how to carry it. It may be foreign to us. It may dominate us. We may have reconciled with it and know how to harness it, but no one is without their shadow. To the contrary, the amount of light we emit is in direct proportion to the size of that shadow. That is a beautiful fucking thing. In our shadow resides our femininity, receptivity, seduction, flow, intuition, sexuality and a large portion of our power. To deny this part of ourselves is to neuter some of our best qualities.

When we stand in rejection of our darkness, this potent creative force will manifest in destructive ways. We end up in relationships with people who carry a disproportionate amount of darkness, engage in addictive behaviors and take unhealthy risks, all of which are the result of imbalance. This is the lesson of the pairs in the tarot: The Magician and The High Priestess, The Empress and The Emperor, The Moon and The Sun. They depict a relationship between light and dark that is in balance, which is what we strive for in relationships and require within ourselves.

So yes, there are cards in the tarot that are dark, difficult and sometimes scary. But if they show up in a reading, it is because that dark energy is already present, whether the person is aware of it or not. The way I read tarot is not based on future prediction. I don't channel information that predicts bad shit happening, so the dark cards are not used in my practice as a way of foretelling doom and disaster. They are a way of honestly revealing the energies at play and painting a full picture of someone's reality. When a dark card presents itself in a reading, I always pull additional cards to show the querist a possible pathway out, or to unearth its roots. That doesn't mean an instant transition to a lighter place, or that facing it is easy, but that is true regardless of whether cards are pulled for them or not.

This is life. It is messy and complicated and profound, and sometimes it fucking sucks. But it is ours to make of it what we choose. And life is too short and too boring to not integrate our darkness in a way that works for us, to feel powerful and in our bodies and to face our deepest truths and fears with thoroughness and integrity. As the kids say, go big or go home, you know?

The Cards in Relationship

Just like our family influences our love lives and our work impacts our personal relationships, a card is not isolated from the cards surrounding it. The Fool in most tarot decks depicts someone about to take a leap. The energy of The Fool is informed by the card they are jumping into. Jumping into The Devil (bondage, addiction) is a much different meaning than jumping into the Ten of Pentacles (wealth, material success) or the Two of Cups (romance, harmony).

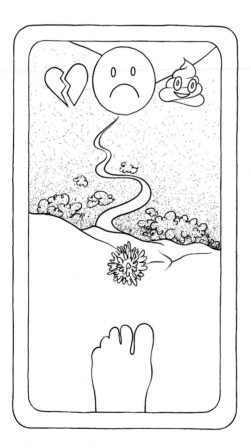

The place in the spread where the card is pulled also heavily contextualizes the cards meaning. To pull a shitty card in the "past" position can mean that a difficult time is over, whereas pulling it in "body" can connote health problems or subconscious burdens. Pulling The Lovers in "spirit" could signify a personal reconciliation, whereas in "future" it can show upcoming partnership, or travel.

As you familiarize yourself with tarot, it will become intuitive to pick up on the general vibe of an entire spread versus the individual meanings of each card that comprises it. This holistic approach is the most successful way not only to understand the reading, but the person receiving it.

Reversed Cards

Many readers use reversed cards in their tarot practice, meaning that when a card is pulled upside down, it possesses an adjusted meaning, versus the meaning it would hold if it were right side up. Typically, reversed cards represent the inverse meaning of the card, and can be read as warnings or perversions of its original energy.

Personally, I do not use reversed cards when I read. I believe that the tarot is an extremely accurate and expansive system in its upright seventy-eight card formation and have not found reversed cards necessary. Additionally, reversed cards create a disproportionate amount of negative possibilities to positive ones, as they traditionally have undesirable meanings. I have never felt like a reading was lacking, or there were not enough possible meanings the cards offered by not using them. I've also been the recipient of some clunky, bummer, inaccurate readings from people struggling to interpret reversed cards. If a positive card is contaminated with a negative force, you will see it in the cards surrounding it. There are cards that both reinforce and oppose each other's meanings, which I detail in their individual descriptions.

While I don't use reversed cards in my readings, the tarot is a large deck of cards, and sometimes shit just comes out upside down. I do not ignore it when it does. In fact, I regard it as especially potent because I don't use them, and if they are presenting themselves in this position then I take it as them really trying to say something. When they do show up, they can speak to an undeveloped energy, something the person isn't seeing or a force that is present but somehow incomplete or unavailable. Basically, a reversed card is a wonky version of its upright counterpart and often presents as a warning.

Boundary Setting & Energetic Protection

While setting boundaries isn't the sexiest topic in the world, it is, in my experience, the most necessary exercise in any magical practice. This is true for many reasons. People are coming for readings in deep vulnerability; they are asking questions and revealing parts of themselves that they oftentimes conceal even from their closest friends. There is a responsibility you hold as a reader to the people coming to you, and the sooner you define your boundaries, the cleaner your practice will be.

When I first started reading tarot, boundaries were a foreign concept to me. I took late night phone calls, confused professional relationships with personal friendships, had no recourse for last minute cancellations, spent unpaid hours responding to e-mails from clients who had follow-up questions, spent a lot of time worrying about what people thought of their readings and feeling guilty if I gave them unwelcome information. Everything I've learned about boundaries over the course of my experience reading tarot is a product of crossing them.

It took time for me to understand boundaries as an act of self-love and self-preservation, and something that makes you and the people around you feel safe. No one enjoys feeling like they are getting something out of obligation, and honoring your boundaries builds a trust that allows people to believe when you say yes, you're all in. I believed that if I said no to something that didn't feel right—a last minute booking that would stretch me too thin, an event opportunity at a loud club full of drunk people on Halloween—I would lose something. It was fear-based decision making that did me no favors besides an expertise in what not to do. Read on.

Dependence and Attachment

While there is nothing more rewarding than working with repeat clients, it is important to stay conscious of the nature of the attachment being formed. Just because someone asks for a reading doesn't mean you need to give it to them, or that it is appropriate at that time. I've had people contact me a week after their last reading asking for another. It is clear, in situations like that, that they either didn't get the answer they wanted or are relying too heavily on the cards to make decisions. Sometimes, people request readings to look into short-term issues that will resolve themselves within days (fight with a partner, a job interview, etc.). I do not offer readings as Band-Aids for panic. To me, it feels exploitative and unethical. I will not capitalize on someone's fear or desperation. There are readers who I love and respect who will do quick reads for people in a pinch, but it does not feel right to me personally. That is my boundary.

Not everyone is happy with me in the moment, but it has built long-term trust with my clients. They know I will not always take their money just because they are willing to give it to me.

Honoring Your Time

Don't get overwhelmed with the idea of charging for readings. You may not be looking to read professionally and therefore exchanging money for readings is not relevant to you. However, to give a reading is an expenditure of energy, and to give energy without receiving anything in return forges an imbalance for both the reader and the querist. When starting out, someone offering their time to help you practice may be exchange enough. However, when you become more comfortable in your ability to give readings, set up some kind of trade with the people coming to you. Money is just energy and by no means the only form of currency. The barter system is a beautiful thing. You can trade a reading for a dinner, a piece of art, a bottle of wine, a massage and the list goes on.

If you are intending to read professionally, it is essential to place monetary value on your time. Oftentimes clients will e-mail after the reading with one more question, or want to follow up on things that came up during the reading. Schedule a follow-up appointment for a pro-rated amount (I offer 15 minute follow-ups) rather than sending a long e-mail or getting on a late night phone call.

It took months of people cancelling appointments at the last minute or not showing up altogether, arguing with me about price and giving follow-up readings for free for me to decide to implement things like a set rate and a cancellation policy. This was scary. Any time we defend our worth—monetary or otherwise—we are probably going to scare the shit out of ourselves a little bit. I already felt like I won the lottery by being able to read tarot professionally and didn't want to push it, but nothing was lost. No one fought me, or questioned it. I didn't lose clients or get wiped off the face of the earth. Same story when I raised my rates, cut down on events and stopped offering in-home readings. Even my fussiest Manhattan clients made the voyage to Brooklyn.

Knowing Your Limitations

The scope of what the tarot can provide a person will never cease to floor me in its expansiveness. The healing and transformation I've seen occur from readings has brought me to tears over and over again. But—and this is a big but—there are indispensable forms of treatment that are not interchangeable with a reading. Chances are you are not a mental health professional. And even if you are, if someone is coming to you for a reading and not counsel on their mental health, then stay in your own lane.

Part of honoring the responsibility others entrust in you is to know when to call it. I've had clients come to me supremely fucked up by readers who gave unsolicited and uninformed advice: recovering addicts told that total sobriety wasn't necessary, people with mental illness advised to get off their medication, cancer patients instructed to change their treatment. I have personal thoughts on all of these matters, but a client isn't coming to you for advice, they are coming for channeled, intuitive guidance.

Sometimes, people just need help beyond a reading's capacity. Anything can come up in a reading—mental illness, childhood trauma, sexual abuse, grief, physical ailments—but that does not mean that you personally have the tools to deal with any and all of these matters. I certainly do not. I do, however, have an arsenal of healers whom I trust and refer people to. This includes therapists, body workers, Reiki practitioners, hypnotists, acupuncturists, mediums, breathworkers, yoga instructors, shamans, intuitives, other tarot readers and, yes, doctors and psychiatrists. If someone's needs exceed your ability to meet them, it is useful to have resources on hand for them and important to guide them to the help they need when you cannot give it. An extreme scenario of this is if someone comes in presenting a danger to themselves or others they should be immediately referred to a physician. Usually, a client will just need ongoing support in continuing their work. Many readers go on to train in additional modalities to provide a more holistic healing experience for their clients and see them through their process.

Self-Care

There is an agreement you make stepping into healership to soften the veil of your ego to truly feel someone else's experience. But once the reading is over, this energy must be released. You are a messenger for the information of the cards, what they deliver to the client is not your fault or your burden. Oftentimes, a reading is just the beginning for a person, as it lays out a map of what they need to do in order to reach their highest potential. This is where the aforementioned resources are a valuable way of further supporting your client in the "now what?" space they sometimes find themselves in. You diminish your usefulness if you hold on to a reading after it is over. Healers have various ways of shaking off excess energy after giving a reading—from prayer and meditation to dancing to taking a bath to going for a walk to watching trashy TV. It doesn't have to be super spiritual; it just has to work for you.

Consent

This one's a biggie, but it is also very simple. If someone doesn't ask for a reading, don't give them one. If you offer someone a reading and they don't explicitly say yes, don't give them one. I've had people come for readings pissed off, skeptical, reluctant, insisting that this was all bullshit. But they still came. They travelled to my space to receive a reading. And, despite their hesitation, when I asked if they wanted to move forward with the reading, they said yes. It's easy to get a little over-enthusiastic at the beginning when we are learning the cards and want to offer them to everyone, and that's largely a positive. But respecting other people's boundaries is paramount to a practice that is rooted in integrity. Only yes means yes, y'all.

Dealing with Assholes

When you tell people that you read tarot, count on some type of response. It's just an interesting and weird and uncommon thing to do, and people almost always have a reaction to it. More often than not, the reaction I've encountered has been enthusiastic and curious, and I've met a lot of clients through organic conversation about what I do. Every once in a very rare while, however, I've encountered people that I like to call assholes who will come at me with various challenges about my job. Here is how I have broken them down.

The Angry Skeptic

"Well you know that's bullshit, right?" is a common response of the Angry Skeptic. This is the only type of asshole that actually gets angry with you when you tell them what you do. It offends their humanistic, materialist sensibilities and, beyond that, threatens their entire conception of reality. They are often armed with irrelevant scientific facts and repeatedly let you know how much they don't believe in this stuff.

How to deal with this type of asshole: Science and magic are not mutually exclusive studies. Galileo believed in astrology, Newton studied alchemy and Einstein touted the importance of intuition in all matters. This makes the Angry Skeptic an easy asshole to take on. There is, invariably, a place where science and hard facts come up short in explaining our universe. Verifiably, scientifically inexplicable phenomenon. When a mystic stands on this edge, they decide to embrace the mystery with faith. Nothing about the act of reading tarot directly refutes science. In fact it plays into String Theory, the idea of a Multiverse and the near-universal agreement that we have not even begun to scratch the surface of this world's mysteries. To pull information from an intangible source and interpret this information through image-based archetypes is certainly not a scientific practice, but it is not one that refutes logic or reason, either. When someone responds with anger to magic, it is because they feel threatened by it. The best way to diffuse this situation is to be as non-threatened as possible. Calmly answer their questions, nod to science when that is relevant and be unwavering but non-aggressive in your beliefs. Once they see they can't rile you up, they usually move on—or ask for a reading.

The Humorously Dismissive

The Dismissive is not too different than the Skeptic, except they don't use anger as a way to make you feel invalid. A bitchy smirk, sarcasm and bad jokes are the weapons of choice for this asshole. They may ask you to predict the upcoming lottery numbers for them, or tell you that they liked magic tricks when they were little, too. In a way these people are worse than the Skeptic because their ways of belittling are more subversive and difficult to detect than outright anger, but it comes from the same place of feeling threatened that you believe in something that they don't.

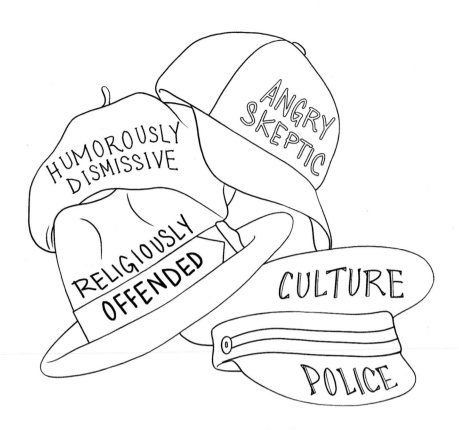

How to deal with this type of asshole: The aim of the Dismissive Asshole is to make you feel like what you are doing is illegitimate. The best way to combat this attempt at making you feel insecure is to remain stubbornly, maddeningly secure. To be apologetic or to minimize what you do is to let them win, which really means that everyone loses, because you feel like shit and they are still an asshole. When I deal with people like this I typically talk about how much I love my job, how lucky I feel that I get to help people all day, that I set my own hours and work on my own terms. I'll talk about all the amazing people I've met and the stories that have moved me and how no two days are ever the same. Then I ask them about their boring-ass job.

Religiously Offended

The Religiously Offended Asshole isn't really an asshole, they just genuinely believe that what you believe stands in opposition to what they do, and they adopt asshole-like tendencies as a result. Unlike the first two assholes, however, they tend to be a bit more earnest in their concern. They just truly believe you're a heathen, or a *bruja*, or otherwise irreconcilably hell-bound. Unlike the previous two assholes, the Religiously Offended actually believes in the power and efficacy of the tarot, but believes it is a plaything of Satan. It says right there in Exodus that, "You shall not permit a sorceress to live." Well, fuck. In addition to being seen as witchcraft, the use of cartomancy could also be seen as worshipping false idols, both of which are biblically problematic practices.

How to deal with these this type of asshole: We have more in common with the religiously offended than might be evident at first glance. The desire is the same: to develop a relationship to Source that we may rely on for support, guidance and community. The only difference is in the approach. While these types of assholes seek out this relationship through organized religion, there are many ways to reach for a connection with Spirit. The cards are a medium between a person and the divine, just as a Priest, Rabbi or Imam Khatib serve as conduits between heaven and earth. We are no more at odds with the Religiously Offended than they are with people of different religions. If what they believe is true and there is only one divine source, then these modalities and rituals are simply different paths to the same mountaintop.

Culture Police

Usually incorrectly overusing phrases like "cultural appropriation" and looking for a fight via social media, the Culture Police are the worst type of asshole. They are quick to call you racist for liking tacos, or listening to rap music. They don't attempt to diminish or discredit the efficacy of the tarot, or harbor genuine concern for the state of your soul. Rather, they hold the position that you do not have the right to a magical practice because it does not belong to you from a cultural standpoint. I've had many uninformed keyboard warriors come at me telling me that magic rightfully belongs to folks of indigenous cultures. While certain mystical practices and religions—Voodoo, Santeria, Native American Medicine—are deeply rooted in culture, there is a way to respectfully and consensually study and practice these magical systems. With tarot, it is a different story.

How to deal with this type of asshole: Knowing the origin of the tarot clears up this type of asshole fairly quickly. Cultural appropriation is defined as members of a dominant group exploiting the culture of marginalized or less privileged groups. The true origin of the tarot is unknown, with the first documented use of it as an esoteric object occurring in France. France is kind of like the ultimate asshole, with a long history of marginalizing and not much of being marginalized. This makes appropriating French culture a near impossible endeavor. Moreover, many different groups, cultures, religions and ethnicities have adopted the tarot and made it their own, which only enhances its power and enriches its story. Magic is available to all. Come to it with humility, with respect, honoring its history, with a genuine desire to learn and it will make itself available to you.

ENHANCING YOUR MAGIC

While the practices discussed in this chapter do not directly correspond to the tarot, they are all ways of enhancing your experience with the cards. Many people find that after beginning to work with their deck, they crave further connection to their intuition and spirituality. Call it a gateway drug. And since healing work is a winding rabbit hole from which there is no return (insert evil laugh here), there are several modalities to aid in providing ritual and deepening your understanding of the tarot.

Developing a ritual around using your cards is a powerful way of shifting into a space where you feel prepared to use them. Ritual is defined as an established or prescribed procedure for a religious or other rite, and you can choose your procedure. Before using my cards, I clean my hands with Florida Water and smudge the deck with white sage. I light a candle, select crystals I feel are appropriate for the client, and ask them to write their name and birthday on a small piece of white paper. I prefer to pull cards on a solid wood surface.

Is everything ruined if I cannot do this? No. I've read at airports on cheap carpeting under fluorescent lights, at events where open flames are not allowed and impromptu at restaurants, on the subway and in nature. The ritual is for the comfort of the reader and creating an atmosphere for the querist. It constructs a safe container, and allows both of us to step out of the daily-grind mindset and into a still, sacred space. It does not, however, impact the efficacy of the cards.

In a reading, huge amounts of information are transmitted, more than the cognitive mind can process in one sitting. There is a point where the brain stops racing to hold it all, allowing for the absorption of the message without ego interference. This is a good thing, but it can also be overwhelming for the recipient of this information overload. Supplementing readings with other types of healing work can soften the experience and help ground the querist.

Chakras

Chakras are the most helpful secondary resource I have found to strengthen my relationship with the cards. A Sanskrit word that means "wheel" or "circle" and referring to the seven main energy centers in the body, each Chakra has a location, color association and mental, emotional and spiritual function. In my deck, the colors in a card will often correspond to the properties of the Chakra associated with it and connect to the card's meaning. Of course this varies from deck to deck. Nonetheless, to isolate areas of the body in order to identify and clear blockages is a useful and accessible tool during readings.

Root Chakra
Color association: dark red
Location: base of spine, legs

The Root Chakra is the energetic command center for our most basic instincts. In a primal sense, it corresponds to food, water and shelter. In a reading, issues in the Root are tied to security, money, grounding and a general sense of feeling safe in the world. Abuse, trauma and financial insecurity will all threaten the stability of this chakra.

Tarot Cards: The Emperor, The Hanged Man, Death,

Sacral Chakra
Color association: orange
Location: pelvis, sex organs

The Sacral Chakra is responsible for sexuality, sensuality, pleasure, enjoyment and passion. It is also the energy center that connects us to our mothers, so needless to say very few of us are damage-free in this area. The feeling of being in the "zone" when doing something you love is connected to the Sacral, as well as feeling comfortable and at home in your body. A disconnect from our bodies, emotions or sexuality will result in blockages in this area.

Tarot Cards: Strength, The Devil, The Moon

Solar Plexus Chakra
Color Association: yellow
Location: upper abdomen

Connected to feelings of personal autonomy, control and confidence, the Solar Plexus is the power center of the ego. People with intact Solar Plexus chakras are unicorns who are well adjusted, set healthy boundaries, and are confident without being pompous. Imbalance will look like aggression, insecurity, paralysis or indecision. Ego strength and ability to be assertive are connected to the Solar Plexus.

Tarot Cards: The Fool, The Chariot, The Sun

Heart Chakra
Color association: green
Location: heart center
Psychic Function: clairsentience

Our Heart Chakra is the gentlest, sweetest energy center of the body. Housing our desires for love, connection, community, joy, peace and vulnerability, the Heart Chakra is rarely unscathed in some way by this life of sin. An intact Heart Chakra will equate vulnerability with strength rather than weakness, open up to others and embrace its needs.

Tarot Cards: The Empress, The Star, The World

Throat Chakra
Color association: blue
Location: throat
Psychic Function: clairaudience

The Throat Chakra manages our voice in all of its manifestations. Our desire to be heard in the world, the clarity of our voice and the integrity of our communication live here. The energetic culmination of the first four chakras is expressed through this one, making any blocks to this area especially volatile. Imbalance will manifest as exploding after keeping things bottled up, or experiencing constriction as a result of self-censorship. A balanced Throat Chakra effectively articulates the person's ideas, thoughts and beliefs.

Tarot Cards: The Magician, The Hierophant, The Lovers

Third Eye Chakra
Color association: purple
Location: between eyebrows
Psychic Function: clairvoyance

Perhaps the most discussed chakra, the Third Eye is known for being the center for our psychic abilities and intuition. An open Third Eye allows perception beyond ordinary sight. Impressions, insights and ability to visualize form here. It also facilitates clear thinking. Imbalance will cause confusion, worry and paranoia.

Tarot Cards: The High Priestess, The Hermit, Justice

Crown Chakra
Color association: white
Location: top of the head and the few inches directly above it
Psychic Function: claircognizance

The Crown Chakra is not connected to any organs or functions in the body the way the other six are. Rather, the Crown allows us to feel a sense of awe, wonder and connectedness to "all that is." It is where matter meets spirit and can be felt most in the moments where we are humbled by the insane perfection of the universe. It infuses in us a bone-level knowing that we are not alone. A blocked Crown Chakra will result in loneliness, victimization and alienation. If overcharged, it will be difficult to ground, identify with your body and feel at home on earth.

Tarot Cards: Temperance, The Tower, Judgment

Crystals

Crystals and gemstones have been lauded for their energetic properties since the beginning of written history. Whether as protective talismans, fertility aids or enhancements of personal power, the intuitive draw people feel with crystals is long-documented and undeniable. You don't have to crack a history book to find evidence of this connection. At Everyday Magic, the heart of the store is a long table covered in crystals, and kids lose their shit over it. I, too, was one of those children. I just never grew out of it. It is safe to say that I am now a full-fledged crystal junkie, and my collection alarms even fellow gemstone enthusiasts.

At the store's opening party, a little boy walked me around the crystal table, picking up stones and intuiting their properties. He was dead on for each one. Aside from reducing me to tears at my own damn party, it reinforced my belief that there is a part of us that knows this already. Of course different stones, depending on where they grew and under what conditions, have specific energetic properties. Of course there is a collective consciousness we can tap into to access this information. Of course magic is real. Duh.

Most crystals correspond to chakras based on their colors and are used for a variety of purposes. Whether holding selenite in your hand for high vibe meditations, keeping a lepidolite or labradorite on your bedside table for restful sleep or lucid dreams, putting an amethyst in the bath for a little bitta bliss, placing citrine on your deck to increase concentration or carrying carnelian in your pocket for an energetic boost, crystals are a simple and beautiful way of enhancing your tarot practice and cultivating a sacred space. There are stones to soothe the nervous system, stimulate cellular repair, facilitate communication, elucidate dreams and call in spirit.

Before pulling cards for a client, I close my eyes and tune in to them. It's a relatively simple process of taking a few deep breaths, letting your own shit fall by the wayside and focusing only on them. You'll often notice sensations or emotions that are not connected to you personally, and it's because, for a moment, you are allowing the other person's energy into your own field. Depending on what I feel from them, I offer a crystal to hold or place one on the table next to them.

If I'm feeling really crazy, I'll lead a client to my crystal shelf and tell them to pull ones they feel drawn to. Once they do, I explain the properties of the stones they chose. There is always a little awakening that occurs upon realizing their choices are completely appropriate for them and what they are going through. If you are a crystal novice, this is how I recommend starting your collection. Choose first, research later. You will not pick the wrong ones.

In the hour I spend with a person, my job is to reflect their power, competence and beauty back to them. That is light work. There are less than scrupulous readers who will edit the information they deliver to cultivate dependence. If you've ever gotten a reading where you heard something like, "Ah yes, you have a dark cloud blocking your third eye chakra, but I will do a ritual on the full moon that will clear it for only $500," then you've experienced that. That, by the way, is bullshit. Choosing crystals intuitively, or letting the people you read for do so, is a small way of illuminating that we already know what we need in order to heal ourselves.

When choosing a crystal, hold it in your left hand and close your eyes. The left side of the body is the feminine, or receptive side. Notice how it feels in your hand, trying to not pay too much attention to aesthetic. My all-time favorite healing stones look like rough, dirt colored little balls. There are some crystals that are truly stunning—the iridescence of labradorite, the gemmy sparkliness of celestite and amethyst, the ocean-like turquoise waves of larimar—but the ugly ducklings of the crystal kingdom are not to be discounted.

Crystals by Chakra
Root: garnet, black tourmaline, smoky quartz
Sacral: carnelian, moqui marbles, shiva lingam
Solar Plexus: citrine, pyrite, golden healer
Heart: rose quartz, malachite, amazonite
Throat: kyanite, larimar, blue lace agate
Third Eye: lapis, amethyst, labradorite
Crown: clear quartz, selenite

Meditation and Intuition
I cannot overstate the importance of meditation not only in reading tarot, but in reducing stress, sharpening intuition, expanding consciousness and improving quality of life in general, which could be why it's so hard to do. Like tarot, meditation can be a daunting proposition for people who don't really know what it is, a cool-kids club for the early-rising, kombucha-drinking yippies who I hate-follow on social media. To an outsider, meditation can feel like taking vitamins—you know you should, but then you're standing in the health food store wondering why some are refrigerated and having a meltdown over how many types of Vitamin B exist.

My dear friend Alex practices Vedic Meditation, a mantra-based technique that leads the mind into a trance state. Similar to the soupy moments between wakefulness and sleep, this form of meditation allows thoughts and images to run through your psyche without being consciously grasped or processed. Alex compares it to a nap, a cup of coffee, a shower or an energetic release depending on her needs at any given time. It has become an essential part of her life, and she will awkwardly meditate on the subway or go into another room when hanging out with people when in need of its restorative properties. She could be cited in a scientific journal about the health benefits of a mindfulness practice because of the immediate, practical results she sees from it. The long-term, positive effects of a general meditation practice are many and can be felt mostly outside of the moments spent in stillness.

While this form of meditation is appealing to me, I lack patience, time and discipline. I am not naturally inclined to sit in stillness, the same way I contemplate breaking one of my arms on purpose when faced with the prospect of going to the gym. And just like it doesn't make sense for someone who has never worked out before to go to a CrossFit class, it is not reasonable for an untrained mind to sit in silent meditation for an extended period of time. My mind is a stir-crazy hamster that requires direction. If I sit in silence I will start obsessing over e-mails, what I want to eat, what does my dog really think about all day, etc.

Rather, I use shorter, guided meditations tailored to an intention. A simple search will yield thousands of results for specific types of meditation—grounding, focus, clarity, restful sleep, stress reduction, body scans—ranging from two minutes to several hours. There are also meditations connected to esoteric and metaphysical practices—chakra healing, past life regression, astral travel and connecting with your spirit guides, and this is where meditation has been an invaluable tool for me. For someone who never considered themselves woo-woo or overtly spiritual, the experiences I've had and things I've seen through this practice have blown my mind over and over again. When I first started meditating, it was with the sole intention of getting to better know my cards. I randomly selected a card out of my deck and gazed at it for several minutes until memorized. I would then close my eyes and visualize myself stepping into the scene of that card and exploring it as a way to further connect with the images.

Since then, I've travelled to seventeenth-century Massachusetts, been taken to an underwater cave and initiated by The High Priestess, communed with ascended masters who informed me they've followed me throughout every lifetime, felt orbs of light enter my body and heal energetic wounds and received messages from the departed. I would not have a fraction of the faith and certainty that I do in the realness of magic if it weren't for my experiences in meditation. Nor, I believe, would I be able to read tarot. The unexpected nature, clarity and precision of what has been revealed to me gave me the confidence to speak my intuition in a reading.

Being a successful reader is contingent upon a strong intuition, with meditation being among the most effective ways to develop it. Regardless of the outlet, meditation is a way of spending unplugged time with yourself. Anything that gets you away from your phone, computer, the constant noise and buzz and low hum of life into your interior landscape will assist in this endeavor. Running, collage, cooking, yoga and gardening can all induce meditative state. The litmus test for the efficacy of your meditation practice is if you can be away from your phone for five minutes without obsessing over whether you got any new likes without wanting to jump out of your skin. If the answer is yes, you're on the right track. It's worth noting that, with the development of intuition, the force of your longing does a lot of the work. To long for something is to manifest it. Again, energy follows intention, and you will find that if the genuine desire is there, the results will follow.

Building Altars

My first altar was a white IKEA shelf, then a windowsill and now a little table on my bedroom floor. An altar is simply a dedicated space for the mindful placement of meaningful objects—the visual expression of a desire. Just like the oven is for cooking (I assume, I've never used mine) or a couch is for nesting and binge-watching Netflix, an altar is for the ritualistic depositing of items that reflect an intention.

It doesn't matter where in your home you put your altar, as long as it is visible to you and cleared for that specific use. One of my girlfriends has an altar on top of her bathroom mirror and it works just fine.

While teaching tarot, I have my students make weekly altars to reflect the card we were studying. I asked that the altar be a physical manifestation of their understanding of that card. For The Empress, which is lush feminine energy, their altars were full of flowers, chocolate, cosmetics, heart chakra crystals, photos of children and mothers, symbols of birth, fertility, creativity, heirlooms passed down from the women in their family. During The Devil week, which is bondage, vices, karmic blockages and addiction, they shared altars housing objects like booze, cigarettes, porn, photos of exes, cash, handcuffs, black and red candles, and symbols of where they felt the most stuck. Every item you put on your altar should hold some meaning and correspond to its theme.

Recently a good friend of mine had a job interview for a position he really wanted. I made an altar for him to support him in getting the job, including Solar Plexus stones, the company's business card, a green candle for abundance, money, yellow flowers, essential oils and tarot cards reflecting professional success and fulfillment—The Chariot, Eight of Pentacles, Ten of Pentacles and Ten of Cups. I built the altar the day he interviewed and kept it up until he heard back about the position.

Yes, he did get the job. Abracadabra, bitches.

I change my altars frequently depending on what's happening in my life at any given time. I recently got out of a long-term relationship and built an altar to support me in finding comfort in aloneness after spending almost a consistent decade in various relationships. It contained photos of friends, mementos of my accomplishments as an individual, books, ticket stubs from trips taken alone and fresh flowers.

If energy follows intention, then making an energetic investment in the form of building an altar is a powerful act of ritual and manifestation. In a perfect world, our whole home is our altar—with each object, whether it be a book or a throw pillow, specifically chosen to energetically support us. William Morris advised, "Have nothing in your house that you do not know to be useful, or believe to be beautiful." Your altar is a physical representation of your spiritual house. Decorate accordingly.

Suggested Altar Items

Crystals

Herbs

Photos

Notes

Tarot cards

Trinkets

Candles

Books

Plants and flowers

Cards/keepsakes

Journaling

Is journaling magic? Why, yes it is. "Words are, in [Dumbledore's] not so humble opinion, our most inexhaustible form of magic." Journaling is a gift that younger us gives present-day us, an opportunity to feel our evolution beyond the capabilities of memory. Read your journal from five years ago, documenting what mattered to you most, how you were feeling, what you were going through, details that would otherwise be forgotten, and then say there is not magic in the act of recording our experiences in this way.

An initiation occurs when you agree to begin a journey with the tarot—a potent esoteric tool with a collective history. I cannot say enough that it is more than the intellectual study. I have been both a student and a teacher of tarot and found this to be true over and over again. Paradigm shifts, changes in consciousness, vivid dreams, profound adjustments in the way we experience and perceive the world are all common occurrences. I journaled religiously during my first year working with the tarot, and every time I read the entries I revisit an amazing, forgotten thing that took place during that time. It is hard for people to see how much they've changed over time, because we spend every day with ourselves and even massive changes occur gradually. It can be similar to meditation insofar as knowing it's a good thing and resisting it anyway, but you rob yourself of clear hindsight by not documenting your initiation. You will thank younger-you later.

The tarot assists in sorting through mental clutter and reaching the heart of the matter—touching on our true motivations and desires. Writing is transference of mind clutter from head to paper, a commitment to yourself and your growth and honoring the worthiness of your experience. It is also worth recording your dreams during this time, as part of the initiation process can happen during sleep, when the veil of the ego is thinnest.

Once you have your deck, fan out the cards in front of you. Sit with each card and let words come to mind. Before you ever pick up a guidebook, (too late, suckaaa!! But seriously, put this book down and do this now) lay out each card and spend a moment with it, writing down any words or feelings that come up. Let your mind be blown when you consult a guidebook and realize you already intuited each card. This, above anything else, will serve as confirmation that we all have some gut-level recognition of these images.

Space Clearing

Similarly to building altars, space clearing is a ritualistic act that helps carve out a sacred container around using your cards. Connected to the belief that dense, residual energies can collect in an environment or object, space clearing is the mindful dispelling of these energies from your space. An energetic—and in some cases a literal—air purifier.

Smudging

Smudging is the ancient art of burning herbs, such as sage, to let the smoke purify and bless a space. It is believed that smudging will clear any lingering negative or heavy energy. Initially used as mystical practice among ancient civilizations, the benefits have since been backed by science. Burning white sage and other herbs releases negative ions, which has been linked to the physical cleansing of a space—clearing mold spores, bacteria, viruses and pollen—as well as its etheric properties.

While the use of smudging with dried white sage originated from Native American practices, the use of burning herb resins (aka incense) for spiritual purposes can be traced as far back as Ancient Egypt. Catholic churches burn incense to symbolize the faithful rising to heaven. It has been used among the Assyrians and Babylonians to ward off evil spirits, and in Judaic Temple rituals. Similarly to tarot, to adopt smudging into your own personal practice is tapping into thousands of years of spiritual communion and ceremony.

The alchemy of smudging is one of turning the earth element (herbs) into the air element (smoke), thereby raising a physical experience into a spiritual one. Smudge sticks can be found at your local health food store, herb shop or metaphysical center. There are also herbalists who craft beautiful, locally sourced smudge sticks available in some gift shops and on sites like Etsy. While the price point is a bit higher, it ensures the ethical sourcing and intentional creation of your smudge stick.

How to use: In a heatproof container, hold a flame to the tip of the smudge stick until it begins to smoke. Using your hand or a feather, guide the smoke into the corners of your space and along the doorways and windows. If using the smoke to cleanse your cards, hold the cards directly above the stream of smoke, fanning them out to make sure each card makes contact. A note of respect for the herbs: This is not an air freshener, people. When you are burning a smudge stick, find a way to honor the earth medicine you are using. Say a prayer or mantra, or silently focus on your intention.

Florida Water

While the word water is in its title, Florida Water is actually an alcohol-based cologne widely lauded for its ability to remove heavy vibrations, protect a home and aid in spiritual cleaning. Named after the fabled fountain of youth purported to exist in Florida (the irony, amirite?), it is scented with essential oils of sweet orange, lemon, lavender and clove. Its bright citrus and floral scent awakens the senses and stimulates the crown chakra, making it an excellent aid in spiritual work.

How to use: Sprinkle some on your hands before handling your cards. Or douse a soft cloth and wipe down your cards for the occasional deep clean. When cleansing your space, add Florida Water to your mopping solution or an all-purpose cleaner.

Singing Bowls

Singing bowls are a form of sound healing that produce tones corresponding to the chakras. The sound induces a feeling of calm, relaxes the nervous system and helps shift both the reader and client into a more peaceful and focused mind-set. There are Tibetan singing bowls, usually forged of metal, and crystal singing bowls, which are made of pure quartz crystal. Some people have full sets of singing bowls, but for personal use and budgetary considerations, try starting with one that corresponds to a chakra you know you want to work on.

Singing bowls are a healing modality in and of themselves, with sound bath offerings available all over the country. However, they are also a powerful supplement to precede a reading or after a particularly intense spread.

Chakra by Musical Note

Root Chakra—C
Sacral Chakra—D
Solar Plexus Chakra—E
Heart Chakra—F
Throat Chakra—G
Third Eye Chakra—A
Crown Chakra—B

How to use: Tap the mallet against the outside edge of the singing bowl, and slowly, without breaking contact, run it along the bowl's perimeter. Experiment with different pressures and speeds to modify the sound. Put your deck of tarot cards inside of the bowl to let the vibrations clear any stuck energy, or use for yourself or a client if feeling nervous before starting a reading.

Salt

The connection between salt and magic has been made repeatedly throughout history. From the Bible to Wiccan practices, its purification properties, healing capacities and the psychic protection it provides makes it an essential ingredient in any witch's spell kit. Bear in mind that salt protects against all psychic phenomena.

Traditionally, witches sprinkled salt across thresholds and around the perimeters of dwellings to ward off outside negative energies, and magical practitioners gather inside circles of salt for both protection and the creation of a safe container. Because of its unique ability to transmit electricity, salt-based crystals are a popular choice to cleanse and amplify both environments and other stones.

How to use: Put a small pile of salt on top of your deck and leave in the sun. Take a salt bath or use a salt scrub to draw out impurities from the body.

— IT'S LIT

COME THROUGH

Sun & Moon

The sun, with is natural antiseptic and antibacterial properties, can be used to cleanse cards, crystals and magic accouterments alike. The moon, with its gentler, ethereal glow, is used to charge.

How to use: Place your sacred objects on a windowsill during a full moon or on a sunny day for natural energization, activation and cleansing.

IT'S BEEN REAL (AND SURREAL)

So, this is it. Everything I know. Every note scribbled on a napkin, every late-night thought typed into my phone, every profound insight I've heard from a student, every possible meaning I've found with each card since I first started using the tarot four years ago. I hope you found it lean but also generous, free of bullshit and ego and at least mildly entertaining. More than anything, I hope you now believe the thing that I believe so strongly that it compelled me to spend six months in a cave writing this fucking thing: that you are ready. Whatever it is, whatever longing is calling out to you in the dark, whatever power and bigness you have yet to harness—you have always had everything you needed in order to begin. All you have to do is say yes.

I hope that, through the tarot, you experience some crazy miraculous shit and are able to make sense of all the crazy miraculous shit that has come to pass. The cards will reflect that life has trained you completely for your healership. I hope you stand a little taller in your specific, perfect place in the universe. I hope there are moments you are so overcome by the presence of magic that you feel like you will break, and then you do break and find you are not broken. I hope you expand exponentially and unendingly. I hope you get your ass kicked by these cards and by life in all the ways you need to in order to be less of an asshole and the truest version of yourself. I hope these cards serve as a vehicle to move you forward and a lens through which you may intentionally view your human experience. I hope it allows to you bask in all of it, to recognize every moment of this life as the nourishment that it is.

Dance with the cards. Learn how to let something else take the lead. Be soft under their touch. They are just and only you.

And you. You are allowed to use magic. It is your birthright. It has always belonged to you.

ACKNOWLEDGMENTS

Thanks first and foremost are owed to Madison Rootenberg and Lilliana Greenway, my two Empresses, whose friendship, support and love falls well beyond the confines of language. To Autumn Whitehurst, my birthday twin and co-pilot in all things magical, as well as her man and my soul-dad Chris McClelland, the most masterful holder of space I've ever known. To my agent, first client and favorite former intern Andrea Morrison: Thank you for holding me from the beginning, with this book being just one of the many milestones you cheerlead me through. To Writers House, thank you for my first and only real job, for letting me hang twinkle lights in the file room, and for growing me up. You guys are second to none in all that you do, including your choice in assistants. Special thanks to Maria Aughavin for being a mother as well as a boss; Melissa Vasquez for being a sister as well as a co-worker; Dan Conaway for being a brilliant albeit unorganized genius; Simon Lipskar for the endless witty banter; and Brianne Johnson for being goals in your authenticity, fierceness and beauty.

To Marissa Giambelluca and the Page Street Publishing team, thank you for reaching out and giving me a) a crazy deadline that tested my sanity in ways I never thought possible and b) an opportunity to share my experience, sass and heart. Thank you for honoring my sometimes offensive voice and guiding me through the manifestation of one of my lifelong dreams.

Kate Scelsa, thank you for one of the most shining cross sections of magic and writing I've ever read, for holding me as I cried the first time we met, for leading me to Sherri and, by extension, absolutely fucking everything. Alex Diamond, Davis Harper, Lindsay Mack, Anna Toonk, Matthew Meier, kudos for making sure this book didn't suck and for generally tolerating my existence.

And last, but certainly not least, to my gorgeous clients, who taught me what the fuck Tarot is and who the fuck I am beyond anyone and anything else.

ABOUT THE AUTHOR
AND ILLUSTRATOR

BAKARA WINTNER is a tarot reader, dog mom, girlboss, writer and owner of Everyday Magic. In her few short years reading tarot, she has gained a reputation as an innately gifted intuitive and reader. Her dynamic and no-nonsense reading style has earned her a vast client base of entrepreneurs, students, CEOs, waiters, celebrities, stay-at-home moms, artists, other healers and a lot of people who don't know what the fuck they're doing. Her readings cover topics including love, career, major life transitions, childhood trauma, couples counseling, grief guidance and inner child healing.

After completing a six-month, immersive study of the Major Arcana with the Brooklyn Fools, she joined founder Jeff Hinshaw as a co-facilitator, offering students an in-depth, experiential journey through the Tarot's archetypes and now teaches group and individual intensives. Trained in Core Energetics therapy and a graduate of Delphi University's In-Depth Channeling program, she pulls across modalities and schools of thought to inform and supplement her readings. She is currently working on her own tarot deck.

Since opening Everyday Magic—an intentional lifestyle shop carrying crystals, tarot cards and ritual objects—Bakara has established herself and her space as a cornerstone of Durham's healing community, where she lives with her pit mix, Zadie Killer.

AUTUMN WHITEHURST has been illustrating for nearly two decades and counts among her clients Coca-Cola, Sapporo, the Principality of Monaco, Ray-Ban, Aveda, BBC and countless magazines, publishers and consumer outlets. She hails from New Orleans but now divides her time between Brooklyn and the rest of the world, this being vital to her creativity and happiness. She's the very best version of herself when she's engaged in messy endeavors and hopes to someday be a bull in its own china shop.

INDEX

0 (The Fool)
  anecdote, 24
  meaning, 23–24
  readings, 25
1 (The Magician)
  anecdote, 26–27
  meaning, 25–26
  readings, 27
2 (The High Priestess)
  anecdote, 29–30
  meaning, 28–29
  readings, 30
3 (The Empress)
  anecdote, 31–32
  meaning, 30–31
  readings, 32
4 (The Emperor)
  anecdote, 34
  meaning, 32–33
  readings, 34
5 (The Hierophant)
  anecdote, 36–37
  meaning, 35–36
  readings, 37
6 (The Lovers)
  anecdote, 39
  meaning, 37–39
  readings, 39
7 (The Chariot)
  anecdote, 41
  meaning, 40–41
  readings, 42
8 (Strength)
  anecdote, 43–44
  meaning, 42–43
  readings, 44
9 (The Hermit)
  anecdote, 45–46
  meaning, 44–45

readings, 46
10 (The Wheel of Fortune)
  anecdote, 48
  meaning, 46–48
  readings, 48–49
11 (Justice)
  anecdote, 50–51
  meaning, 49–50
  readings, 51
12 (The Hanged Man)
  anecdote, 53
  meaning, 51–53
  readings, 53–54
13 (Death)
  anecdote, 55–56
  meaning, 54–55
  readings, 56
14 (Temperance)
  anecdote, 58
  meaning, 56–58
  readings, 58
15 (The Devil)
  anecdote, 60–61
  Major Arcana, 59–61
  meaning, 59–60
  readings, 61
16 (The Tower)
  anecdote, 63–64
  meaning, 62–63
  readings, 64
17 (The Star)
  anecdote, 65–66
  meaning, 64–65
  readings, 66
18 (The Moon)
  anecdote, 68
  meaning, 66–68
  readings, 68
19 (The Sun)

anecdote, 70
meaning, 69–70
readings, 71
20 (Judgment)
  anecdote, 73
  meaning, 71–73
  readings, 73–74
21 (The World)
  anecdote, 75–76
  meaning, 74–75
  readings, 76

Ace of Cups, 89–90
Ace of Pentacles, 95–96
Ace of Swords, 83–84
Ace of Wands, 78–79
Advanced Magick for Beginners (Alan Chapman), 18
Adyashanti, 61
Alex, 143
altars, 145–146
anecdotes
  The Chariot (7), 41
  Death (13), 55–56
  The Devil (15), 60–61
  The Emperor (4), 34
  The Empress (3), 31–32
  The Fool (0), 24
  The Hanged Man (12), 53
  The Hermit (9), 45–46
  The Hierophant (5), 36–37
  The High Priestess (2), 29–30
  Judgment (20), 73
  Justice (11), 50–51
  The Lovers (6), 39
  The Magician (1), 26–27

The Moon (18), 68
The Star (17), 65–66
Strength (8), 43–44
The Sun (19), 70
Temperance (14), 58
The Tower (16), 63–64
The Wheel of Fortune
(10), 48
The World (21), 75–76
"Angels" (Chance the Rapper), 56
artists, 19, 20
Autumn, 101

Bembo, Bonifacio, 12
Beyoncé, 40
Bright Eyes, 51

Campbell, Joseph, 44
cards
artists and, 19, 20
feminine energy, 21–22
honesty of, 13
imagery of, 14
masculine energy, 21–22
origin of, 12, 13, 137
pulling, 126
relationships between, 131
reversed cards, 131
shuffling, 126
Chakras
Crown Chakra, 141, 143,
149
Heart Chakra, 140, 143,
149
introduction to, 139
musical notes and, 149
Root Chakra, 139, 143,
149
Sacral Chakra, 139, 143,
149
Solar Plexus Chakra, 139,
143, 149

Third Eye Chakra, 141,
143, 149
Throat Chakra, 141, 143,
149
Chakra Spread, 123
Chance the Rapper, 56
Chapman, Alan, 18
The Chariot (7)
anecdote, 41
meaning, 40–41
readings, 42
Chris, 101
consent, 134
Court Cards
Daughter of Cups, 112
Daughter of Pentacles,
116–117
Daughter of Swords,
108–109
Daughter of Wands,
104–105
Father of Cups, 114–115
Father of Pentacles, 118
Father of Swords, 111
Father of Wands, 107–108
introduction to, 103–104
Mother of Cups, 114
Mother of Pentacles,
117–118
Mother of Swords,
110–111
Mother of Wands,
106–107
Son of Cups, 113–114
Son of Pentacles, 117
Son of Swords, 109–110
Son of Wands, 105–106
Court de Gébelin, Antoine,
12
Crackerjack, 101
Crowley, Aleister, 12
Crown Chakra, 141, 143,
149

crystals, 142–143
Cups
Ace of Cups, 89–90
Two of Cups, 90
Three of Cups, 91
Four of Cups, 91
Five of Cups, 91–92
Six of Cups, 92
Seven of Cups, 92–93
Eight of Cups, 93–94
Nine of Cups, 94
Ten of Cups, 94
Daughter of Cups, 112
Father of Cups, 114–115
Mother of Cups, 114
Son of Cups, 113–114

Daughter of Cups, 112
Daughter of Pentacles,
116–117
Daughter of Swords,
108–109
Daughter of Wands,
104–105
Death (13)
anecdote, 55–56
meaning, 54–55
readings, 56
decks
Fountain Tarot, 19
gifts of, 20
indie decks, 19
Lumina Tarot, 19
purchasing, 20
Rider-Waite Tarot, 12, 19
selection, 19–20
Small Spells Tarot, 19
Spirit Speak Tarot, 19
Starchild Tarot, 19
Thoth Tarot, 12
Visconti Tarot, 12
Wooden Tarot, 19

The Devil (15)
anecdote, 60–61
Major Arcana, 59–61
meaning, 59–60
readings, 61

Eight of Cups, 93–94
Eight of Pentacles, 100
Eight of Swords, 87
Eight of Wands, 82
Einstein, Albert, 27
Ellipse Spread, 122–123
The Emperor (4)
anecdote, 34
meaning, 32–33
readings, 34
The Empress (3)
anecdote, 31–32
meaning, 30–31
readings, 32
Everyday Magic, 17, 50–51, 70, 76
Everything Spread, 120–121

Father of Cups, 114–115
Father of Pentacles, 118
Father of Swords, 111
Father of Wands, 107–108
feminine energy, 21–22
Five of Cups, 91–92
Five of Pentacles, 98
Five of Swords, 86
Five of Wands, 80–81
Florida Water, 149
The Fool (0)
anecdote, 24
meaning, 23–24
readings, 25
"Formation" (Beyoncé), 40
Fountain Tarot, 19
Four of Cups, 91
Four of Pentacles, 97

Four of Swords, 85–86
Four of Wands, 80

Gaiman, Neil, 64
gemstones, 142–143

Hafiz, 42
The Hanged Man (12)
anecdote, 53
meaning, 51–53
readings, 53–54
Heart Chakra, 140, 143, 149
Hermetic Order of the Golden Dawn, 12
The Hermit (9)
anecdote, 45–46
meaning, 44–45
readings, 46
The Hierophant (5)
anecdote, 36–37
meaning, 35–36
readings, 37
The High Priestess (2)
anecdote, 29–30
meaning, 28–29
readings, 30

intuition, 144

Jenna, 63
Jodorowsky, Alejandro, 15
journaling, 147
Judgment (20)
anecdote, 73
meaning, 71–73
readings, 73–74
Jung, Carl, 23
Justice (11)
anecdote, 50–51
meaning, 49–50
readings, 51

Letters to a Young Poet (Rainer Maria Rilke), 37
Lisa, 8–9
The Lovers (6)
anecdote, 39
meaning, 37–39
readings, 39
Lumina Tarot, 19

Madison, 70
magic
altars, 145–146
association as, 16–17
Crown Chakra, 141, 143, 149
crystals, 142–143
Florida Water, 149
gemstones, 142–143
Heart Chakra, 140, 143, 149
introduction to, 16–18
journaling, 147
meditation, 143
moon, 150
perception of, 16
Root Chakra, 139, 143, 149
Sacral Chakra, 139, 143, 149
salt, 150
singing bowls, 149
smudging, 148
Solar Plexus Chakra, 139, 143, 149
space clearing, 148–150
sun, 150
Third Eye Chakra, 141, 143, 149
Throat Chakra, 141, 143, 149
Vedic Meditation, 143–144

The Magician (1)
  anecdote, 26–27
  meaning, 25–26
  readings, 27
Major Arcana
  The Chariot (7), 40–42
  Death (13), 54–56
  The Devil (15), 59–61
  The Emperor (4), 32–34
  The Empress (3), 30–32
  The Fool (0), 23–25
  The Hanged Man (12),
    51–54
  The Hermit (9), 44–46
  The Hierophant (5),
    35–37
  The High Priestess (2), 27
  Judgment (20), 71–74
  Justice (11), 49–51
  The Lovers (6), 37–39
  The Magician (1), 25–27
  The Moon (18), 66–68
  The Star (17), 64–66
  Strength (8), 42–44
  The Sun (19), 69–71
  Temperance (14), 56–58
  The Tower (16), 61–64
  The Wheel of Fortune
    (10), 46–49
  The World (21), 74–76
masculine energy, 21–22
meaning
  The Chariot (7), 40–41
  Death (13), 54–55
  The Devil (15), 59–60
  The Emperor (4), 32–33
  The Empress (3), 30–31
  The Fool (0), 23–24
  The Hanged Man (12),
    51–53
  The Hermit (9), 44–45
  The Hierophant (5),
    35–36

The High Priestess (2),
  28–29
Judgment (20), 71–73
Justice (11), 49–50
The Lovers (6), 37–39
The Magician (1), 25–26
The Moon (18), 66–68
The Star (17), 64–65
Strength (8), 42–43
The Sun (19), 69–70
Temperance (14), 56–58
The Tower (16), 62–63
The Wheel of Fortune
  (10), 46–48
The World (21), 74–75
meditation, 143
"Middleman" (Bright Eyes),
  51
Milos, 29–30
Minor Arcana
  Ace of Cups, 89–90
  Ace of Pentacles, 95–96
  Ace of Swords, 83–84
  Ace of Wands, 78–79
  Two of Cups, 90
  Two of Pentacles, 96
  Two of Swords, 84
  Two of Wands, 79
  Three of Cups, 91
  Three of Pentacles, 96–97
  Three of Swords, 85
  Three of Wands, 79–80
  Four of Cups, 91
  Four of Pentacles, 97
  Four of Swords, 85–86
  Four of Wands, 80
  Five of Cups, 91–92
  Five of Pentacles, 98
  Five of Swords, 86
  Five of Wands, 80–81
  Six of Cups, 92
  Six of Pentacles, 99
  Six of Swords, 86

Six of Wands, 81
Seven of Cups, 92–93
Seven of Pentacles, 99
Seven of Swords, 87
Seven of Wands, 82
Eight of Cups, 93–94
Eight of Pentacles, 100
Eight of Swords, 87
Eight of Wands, 82
Nine of Cups, 94
Nine of Pentacles,
  100–101
Nine of Swords, 88
Nine of Wands, 82
Ten of Cups, 94
Ten of Pentacles, 101–102
Ten of Swords, 88–89
Ten of Wands, 83
moon, magic and, 150
The Moon (18)
  anecdote, 68
  meaning, 66–68
  readings, 68
Morris, William, 145
Mother of Cups, 114
Mother of Pentacles,
  117–118
Mother of Swords, 110–111
Mother of Wands, 106–107

Nejma (Nayyirah Waheed),
  54
Nine of Cups, 94
Nine of Pentacles, 100–101
Nine of Swords, 88
Nine of Wands, 82

origin, 12, 13, 137

Peace (Gene Wolf), 69
Pentacles
  Ace of Pentacles, 95–96
  Two of Pentacles, 96

Three of Pentacles, 96–97
Four of Pentacles, 97
Five of Pentacles, 98
Six of Pentacles, 99
Seven of Pentacles, 99
Eight of Pentacles, 100
Nine of Pentacles,
    100–101
Ten of Pentacles, 101–102
Daughter of Pentacles,
    116–117
Father of Pentacles, 118
Mother of Pentacles,
    117–118
Son of Pentacles, 117
PipSqueak, 101
Pope, Olivia, 25

Rama (swami), 35
readings
    boundaries, 132
    card relationships,
        130–131
    The Chariot (7), 42
    client attachment, 132
    consent for, 134
    cultural appropriation and,
        137
    daily draw, 128
    Death (13), 56
    The Devil (15), 61
    difficult cards, 129–130
    dismissiveness and,
        135–136
    The Emperor (4), 34
    The Empress (3), 32
    finishing, 127
    follow-up conversations,
        133
    The Fool (0), 25
    The Hanged Man (12),
        53–54
    The Hermit (9), 46
    The Hierophant (5), 37

The High Priestess (2), 30
    introduction to, 124
    intuition and, 144
    Judgment (20), 73–74
    Justice (11), 51
    length of, 127
    limitations and, 133–134
    The Lovers (6), 39
    The Magician (1), 27
    The Moon (18), 68
    opening conversations,
        125, 126
    payment for, 133
    pulling cards for, 126
    pushback, 127–128
    religious beliefs and,
        136–137
    reversed cards, 131
    self-care and, 134
    self-readings, 128
    shuffling, 126
    skeptics and, 135
    The Star (17), 66
    Strength (8), 44
    The Sun (19), 71
    Temperance (14), 58
    The Tower (16), 64
    The Wheel of Fortune
        (10), 48–49
    The World (21), 76
religion, 136–137
reversed cards, 131
Rider-Waite Tarot, 12, 19
Rilke, Rainer Maria, 37
Root Chakra, 139, 143, 149

Sacral Chakra, 139, 143,
    149
salt, 150
self-care, 134
self-readings, 128
Seven of Cups, 92–93
Seven of Pentacles, 99
Seven of Swords, 87

Seven of Wands, 82
Sherri, 7–8, 9, 36–37
shuffling, 126
singing bowls, 149
Six of Cups, 92
Six of Pentacles, 99
Six of Swords, 86
Six of Wands, 81
skeptics, 135
Small Spells Tarot, 19
smudging, 148
Solar Plexus Chakra, 139,
    143, 149
Son of Cups, 113–114
Son of Pentacles, 117–118
Son of Swords, 109–110
Son of Wands, 105–106
space clearing, 148–150
Spirit Speak Tarot, 19
spreads
    card relationships and, 131
    Chakra Spread, 123
    Ellipse Spread, 122–123
    Everything Spread,
        120–121
    introduction to, 119
The Star (17)
    anecdote, 65–66
    meaning, 64–65
    readings, 66
Starchild Tarot, 19
Stardust (Neil Gaiman), 64
Strayed, Cheryl, 71
Strength (8)
    anecdote, 43–44
    meaning, 42–43
    readings, 44
sun, magic and, 150
The Sun (19)
    anecdote, 70
    meaning, 69–70
    readings, 71
Swami Rama of the Himalayas,
    35

Swords
  Ace of Swords, 83–84
  Two of Swords, 84
  Three of Swords, 85
  Four of Swords, 85–86
  Five of Swords, 86
  Six of Swords, 86
  Seven of Swords, 87
  Eight of Swords, 87
  Nine of Swords, 88
  Ten of Swords, 88–89
  Daughter of Swords,
      108–109
  Father of Swords, 111
  Mother of Swords,
      110–111
  Son of Swords, 109–110

tarot cards
  artists and, 19, 20
  feminine energy, 21–22
  honesty of, 13
  imagery of, 14
  masculine energy, 21–22
  origin of, 12, 13, 137
  pulling, 126
  relationships between, 131
  reversed cards, 131
  shuffling, 126
tarot decks
  Fountain Tarot, 19
  gifts of, 20
  indie decks, 19
  Lumina Tarot, 19
  purchasing, 20
  Rider-Waite Tarot, 12, 19
  selection, 19–20
  Small Spells Tarot, 19
  Spirit Speak Tarot, 19
  Starchild Tarot, 19
  Thoth Tarot, 12
  Visconti Tarot, 12
  Wooden Tarot, 19

tarot spreads
  card relationships and, 131
  Chakra Spread, 123
  Ellipse Spread, 122–123
  Everything Spread,
      120–121
  introduction to, 119
Temperance (14)
  anecdote, 58
  meaning, 56–58
  readings, 58
Ten of Cups, 94
Ten of Pentacles, 101–102
Ten of Swords, 88–89
Ten of Wands, 83
Third Eye Chakra, 141, 143,
      149
Thoreau, Henry David, 66
Thoth Tarot, 12
Three of Cups, 91
Three of Pentacles, 96–97
Three of Swords, 85
Three of Wands, 79–80
Throat Chakra, 141, 143, 149
Tiny Beautiful Things:
      Advice on Love and
      Life from Dear Sugar
      (Cheryl Strayed), 71
Tootoosis, Gordon, 32
The Tower (16)
  anecdote, 63–64
  meaning, 62–63
  readings, 64
Two of Cups, 90
Two of Pentacles, 96
Two of Swords, 84
Two of Wands, 79

Vedic Meditation, 143–144
Visconti-Sforza family, 12
Visconti Tarot, 12
Waheed, Nayyirah, 54
Waite, Arthur Edward, 12

Walden (Henry David Tho-
      reau), 66
Wands
  Ace of Wands, 78–79
  Two of Wands, 79
  Three of Wands, 79–80
  Four of Wands, 80
  Five of Wands, 80–81
  Six of Wands, 81
  Seven of Wands, 82
  Eight of Wands, 82
  Nine of Wands, 82
  Ten of Wands, 83
  Daughter of Wands,
      104–105
  Father of Wands, 107–108
  Mother of Wands,
      106–107
  Son of Wands, 105–106
The Way of the Tarot (Ale-
      jandro Jodorowsky),
      15
The Wheel of Fortune (10)
  anecdote, 48
  meaning, 46–48
  readings, 48–49
Wolf, Gene, 69
Wooden Tarot, 19
The World (21)
  anecdote, 75–76
  meaning, 74–75
  readings, 76

Zadie Killer, 34, 55–56, 75